WORD BY WORD

Second Edition

PICTURE DICTIONARY

Steven J. Molinsky • Bill Bliss

Illustrated by
Richard E. Hill

Longman

longman.com

Dedicated to Janet Johnston in honor of her wonderful contribution
to the development of our textbooks over three decades.

Steven J. Molinsky
Bill Bliss

Word by Word Picture Dictionary, second edition

Pearson Education, 10 Bank Street, White Plains, NY 10606

Editorial director: Pam Fishman
Vice president, director of design and production: Rhea Banker
Director of electronic production: Aliza Greenblatt
Director of manufacturing: Patrice Fraccio
Senior manufacturing manager: Edith Pullman
Marketing manager: Oliva Fernandez
Senior digital layout specialist: Wendy Wolf
Text design: Wendy Wolf
Cover design: Tracey Munz Cataldo
Realia creation: Warren Fischbach, Paula Williams
Illustrations: Richard E. Hill
Contributing artists: Steven Young, Charles Cawley, Willard Gage, Marlon Violette
WordSongs Music CD: Peter S. Bliss

Additional photos/illustrations: Pages **162** *top* **163** *middle* U.S. National Archives &
Records Administration

Library of Congress Control Number: 2005923423

ISBN 0-13-235838-7; 978-0-13-235838-5
Pearson Longman on the Web
Pearson Longman.com offers online resources for teachers and students. Access our Companion Websites,
our online catalog, and our local offices around the world.

Visit us at longman.com.

Printed in the United States of America
5 6 7 8 9 10 – RRD – 12 11 10 09

CONTENTS

Unit / Theme	Communication Skills	Writing & Discussion	CASAS	LAUSD	LCPs
1 Personal Information and Family	• Asking for & giving personal information • Identifying information on a form • Spelling name aloud • Identifying family members • Introducing others	• Telling about yourself • Telling about family members • Drawing a family tree	0.1.2, 0.1.4, 0.2.1, 0.2.2	*Beg. Low:* 1, 2, 4, 6, 7, 9, 58 *Beg. High:* 1, 4, 5, 6 *Interm. Low:* 1	LCP A: 05, 14, 15 LCP B: 22, 31 LCP C: 39 LCP D: 56
2 Common Everyday Activities and Language	• Identifying classroom objects & locations • Identifying classroom actions • Giving & following simple classroom commands • Identifying everyday & leisure activities • Inquiring by phone about a person's activities • Asking about a person's plan for future activities • Social communication: Greeting people, Leave taking, Introducing yourself & others, Getting someone's attention, Expressing gratitude, Saying you don't understand, Calling someone on the telephone • Describing the weather • Interpreting temperatures on a thermometer (Fahrenheit & Centigrade) • Describing the weather forecast for tomorrow	• Describing a classroom • Making a list of daily activities • Describing daily routine • Making a list of planned activities • Describing favorite leisure activities • Describing the weather	0.1.1, 0.1.2, 0.1.4, 0.1.5, 0.1.6, 0.2.1, 0.2.4, 1.1.5, 2.1.8, 2.3.3, 7.5.5, 7.5.6, 8.2.3, 8.2.5	*Beg. Low:* 9, 11, 12, 13, 15, 18, 28, 29 *Beg. High:* 7a, 7b, 11, 15, 26 *Interm. Low:* 4a, 5	LCP A: 05, 06, 13 LCP B: 22, 30 LCP C: 39, 47 LCP D: 56, 57
3 Numbers/ Time/ Money/ Calendar	• Using cardinal & ordinal numbers • Giving information about age, number of family members, residence • Telling time • Indicating time of events • Asking for information about arrival & departure times • Identifying coins & currency – names & values • Making & asking for change • Identifying days of the week • Identifying months of the year • Asking about the year, month, day, date • Asking about the date of a birthday, anniversary, appointment • Giving date of birth	• Describing numbers of students in a class • Identifying a country's population • Describing daily schedule with times • Telling about time management • Telling about the use of time in different cultures or countries • Describing the cost of purchases • Describing coins & currency of other countries • Describing weekday & weekend activities • Telling about favorite day of the week & month of the year	0.1.2, 0.2.1, 1.1.6, 2.3.1, 2.3.2	*Beg. Low:* 3, 4, 25, 26, 30 *Beg. High:* 2, 5	LCP A: 08 LCP B: 25 LCP C: 42
4 Home	• Identifying types of housing & communities • Requesting a taxi • Calling 911 for an ambulance • Identifying rooms of a home • Identifying furniture • Complimenting • Asking for information in a store • Locating items in a store • Asking about items on sale • Asking the location of items at home • Telling about past weekend activities • Identifying locations in an apartment building • Identifying ways to look for housing: classified ads, listings, vacancy signs • Renting an apartment • Describing household problems • Securing home repair services • Making a suggestion • Identifying household cleaning items, home supplies, & tools • Asking to borrow an item • Describing current home activities & plans for future activities	• Describing types of housing where people live • Describing rooms & furniture in a residence • Telling about baby products & early child-rearing practices in different countries • Telling about personal experiences with repairing things • Describing an apartment building • Describing household cleaning chores	0.1.2, 0.1.4, 1.4.1, 1.4.2, 1.4.7, 2.1.2, 7.5.5, 8.2.5, 8.2.6	*Beg. Low:* 12, 13, 21, 38, 39 *Beg. High:* 10c, 20, 37, 38, 39 *Interm. Low:* 3, 4c, 4e, 4f, 22	LCP A: 04, 06, 11 LCP B: 21 LCP C: 38, 40, 45 LCP D: 55, 62
5 Community	• Identifying places in the community • Exchanging greetings • Asking & giving the location of places in the community • Identifying government buildings, services, & other places in a city/town center • Identifying modes of transportation in a city/town center	• Describing places in a neighborhood • Making a list of places, people, & actions observed at an intersection	0.1.2, 0.1.4, 2.5.3, 2.5.4	*Beg. Low:* 22, 23, 24 *Beg. High:* 23	LCP A: 05, 12 LCP B: 29 LCP C: 46 LCP D: 56

CASAS: Comprehensive Adult Student Assessment System
LAUSD: Los Angeles Unified School District content standards (Beginning Low, Beginning High, Intermediate Low)
LCPs: Literacy Completion Points – Florida & Texas workforce development skills & life skills (Levels A, B, C, D)

Unit / Theme	Communication Skills	Writing & Discussion	CASAS	LAUSD	LCPs
6 Describing	• Describing people by age • Describing people by physical characteristics • Describing a suspect or missing person to a police officer • Describing people & things using adjectives • Describing physical states & emotions • Expressing concern about another person's physical state or emotion	• Describing physical characteristics of yourself & family members • Describing physical characteristics of a favorite actor or actress or other famous person • Describing things at home & in the community • Telling about personal experiences with different emotions	0.1.2, 0.2.1	*Beg. Low:* 6 *Beg. High:* 3, 7b	LCP A: 05 LCP B: 22 LCP C: 39, 49 LCP D: 56
7 Food	• Identifying food items (fruits, vegetables, meat, poultry, seafood, dairy products, juices, beverages, deli, frozen foods, snack foods, groceries) • Identifying non-food items purchased in a supermarket (e.g., household supplies, baby products, pet food) • Determining food needs to make a shopping list • Asking the location of items in a supermarket • Identifying supermarket sections • Requesting items at a service counter in a supermarket • Identifying supermarket checkout area personnel & items • Identifying food containers & quantities • Identifying units of measure • Asking for & giving recipe instructions • Complimenting someone on a recipe • Offering to help with food preparation • Identifying food preparation actions • Identifying kitchen utensils & cookware • Asking to borrow an item • Comprehending product advertising • Ordering fast food items, coffee shop items, & sandwiches • Indicating a shortage of supplies to a co-worker or supervisor • Taking customers' orders at a food service counter • Identifying restaurant objects, personnel, & actions • Making & following requests at work • Identifying & correctly positioning silverware & plates in a table setting • Inquiring in person about restaurant job openings • Ordering from a restaurant menu • Taking customers' orders as a waiter or waitress in a restaurant	• Describing favorite & least favorite foods • Describing foods in different countries • Making a shopping list • Describing places to shop for food • Telling about differences between supermarkets & food stores in different countries • Making a list of items in kitchen cabinets & the refrigerator • Describing recycling practices • Describing a favorite recipe using units of measure • Telling about use of kitchen utensils & cookware • Telling about experience with different types of restaurants • Describing restaurants and menus in different countries • Describing favorite foods ordered in restaurants	0.1.2, 0.1.4, 1.1.1, 1.1.7, 1.3.7, 1.3.8, 2.6.4, 4.8.3	*Beg. Low:* 14, 32, 35, 37 *Beg. High:* 10c, 30, 31, 34, 36 *Interm. Low:* 4c, 4e	LCP A: 05, 07, 11 LCP B: 24, 28 LCP C: 45
8 Colors and Clothing	• Identifying colors • Complimenting someone on clothing • Identifying clothing items, including outerwear, sleepwear, underwear, exercise clothing, footwear, jewelry, & accessories • Talking about appropriate clothing for different weather conditions • Expressing clothing needs to a store salesperson • Locating clothing items • Inquiring about ownership of found clothing items • Indicating loss of a clothing item • Asking about sale prices in a clothing store • Reporting theft of a clothing item to the police • Stating preferences during clothing shopping • Expressing problems with clothing & the need for alterations • Identifying laundry objects & activities • Locating laundry products in a store	• Describing the flags of different countries • Telling about emotions associated with different colors • Telling about clothing & colors you like to wear • Describing clothing worn at different occasions (e.g., going to schools, parties, weddings) • Telling about clothing worn in different weather conditions • Telling about clothing worn during exercise activities • Telling about footwear worn during different activities • Describing the color, material, size, & pattern of favorite clothing items • Comparing clothing fashions now & a long time ago • Telling about who does laundry at home	0.1.2, 0.1.4, 1.1.9, 1.2.1, 1.3.7, 1.3.9, 8.2.4	*Beg. Low:* 14, 31, 32, 33, 34 *Beg. High:* 10c, 30, 33 *Interm. Low:* 4e, 20, 21	LCP A: 05, 11, 15 LCP B: 28 LCP C: 45 LCP D: 56

Unit / Theme	Communication Skills	Writing & Discussion	CASAS	LAUSD	LCPs
9 Shopping	• Identifying departments & services in a department store • Asking the location of items in a department store • Asking to buy, return, exchange, try on, & pay for department store items • Asking about regular & sales prices, discounts, & sales tax • Interpreting a sales receipt • Offering assistance to customers as a salesperson • Expressing needs to a salesperson in a store • Identifying electronics products, including video & audio equipment, telephones, cameras, & computers • Identifying components of a computer & common computer software • Complimenting someone about an item & inquiring where it was purchased • Asking a salesperson for advice about different brands of a product • Identifying common toys & other items in a toy store • Asking for advice about an appropriate gift for a child	• Describing a department store • Telling about stores that have sales • Telling about an item purchased on sale • Comparing different types & brands of video & audio equipment • Describing telephones & cameras • Describing personal use of a computer • Sharing opinions about how computers have changed the world • Telling about popular toys in different countries • Telling about favorite childhood toys	0.1.2, 0.1.3, 0.1.4, 1.2.2, 1.2.3, 1.3.3, 1.3.7, 1.6.3, 1.6.4, 4.8.3	*Beg. Low:* 31, 32 *Beg. High:* 10c, 30, 60 *Interm. Low:* 4d, 4e, 4h, 20, 21, 37	*LCP B:* 28 *LCP C:* 45 *LCP D:* 56
10 Community Services	• Requesting bank services & transactions (e.g., deposit, withdrawal, cashing a check, obtaining traveler's checks, opening an account, applying for a loan, exchanging currency) • Identifying bank personnel • Identifying bank forms • Asking about acceptable forms of payment (cash, check, credit card, money order, traveler's check) • Identifying household bills (rent, utilities, etc.) • Identifying family finance documents & actions • Following instructions to use an ATM machine • Requesting post office services & transactions • Identifying types of mail & mail services • Identifying different ways to buy stamps • Requesting non-mail services available at the post office (money order, selective service registration, passport application) • Identifying & locating library sections, services, & personnel • Asking how to find a book in the library • Identifying community institutions, services, and personnel (police, fire, city government, public works, recreation, sanitation, religious institutions) • Identifying types of emergency vehicles • Reporting a crime • Identifying community mishaps (gas leak, water main break, etc.) • Expressing concern about community problems	• Describing use of bank services • Telling about household bills & amounts paid • Telling about the person responsible for household finances • Describing use of ATM machines • Describing use of postal services • Comparing postal systems in different countries • Telling about experience using a library • Telling about the location of community institutions • Describing experiences using community institutions • Telling about crime in the community • Describing experience with a crime or emergency	0.1.2, 1.3.1, 1.3.3, 1.4.4, 1.5.1, 1.5.3, 1.8.1, 1.8.2, 1.8.4, 2.4.1, 2.4.2, 2.4.4, 2.5.1, 2.5.4, 2.5.6, 5.6.1, 8.2.1	*Beg. Low:* 8 *Beg. High:* 24, 28, 29 *Interm. Low:* 16, 19, 23, 26	*LCP A:* 08, 11, 12 *LCP B:* 25, 28, 29 *LCP C:* 42, 44, 46 *LCP D:* 59, 61
11 Health	• Identifying parts of the body & key internal organs • Describing ailments, symptoms, & injuries • Asking about the health of another person • Identifying items in a first-aid kit • Describing medical emergencies • Identifying emergency medical procedures (CPR, rescue breathing, Heimlich maneuver) • Calling 911 to report a medical emergency • Identifying major illnesses • Talking with a friend or co-worker about illness in one's family • Following instructions during a medical examination • Identifying medical personnel, equipment, & supplies in medical & dental offices • Understanding medical & dental personnel's description of procedures during treatment • Understanding a doctor's medical advice and instructions • Identifying over-the-counter medications • Understanding dosage instructions on medicine labels • Identifying medical specialists • Indicating the date & time of a medical appointment • Identifying hospital departments & personnel • Identifying equipment in a hospital room • Identifying actions & items related to personal hygiene • Locating personal care products in a store • Identifying actions & items related to baby care	• Describing self • Telling about a personal experience with an illness or injury • Describing remedies or treatments for common problems (cold, stomachache, insect bite, hiccups) • Describing experience with a medical emergency • Describing a medical examination • Describing experience with a medical or dental procedure • Telling about medical advice received • Telling about over-the-counter medications used • Comparing use of medications in different countries • Describing experience with a medical specialist • Describing a hospital stay • Making a list of personal care items needed for a trip • Comparing baby products in different countries	0.1.2, 0.1.4, 1.3.7, 2.1.2, 2.5.3, 2.5.9, 3.1.1, 3.1.2, 3.1.3, 3.3.1, 3.3.2, 3.3.3, 3.4.2, 3.4.3, 3.5.4, 3.5.5, 3.5.9, 8.1.1	*Beg. Low:* 12, 21, 32, 43, 44, 45, 46 *Beg. High:* 10b, 20, 30, 43, 45, 46, 47, 50 *Interm. Low:* 4g, 27, 28, 30	*LCP A:* 06, 07, 10, 14 *LCP B:* 24, 27 *LCP C:* 40, 41, 44, 48 *LCP D:* 56, 58

Unit / Theme	Communication Skills	Writing & Discussion	CASAS	LAUSD	LCPs
12 School, Subjects, and Activities	• Identifying types of educational institutions • Giving information about previous education during a job interview • Identifying school locations & personnel • Identifying school subjects • Identifying extracurricular activities • Sharing after-school plans • MATH: • Asking & answering basic questions during a math class • Using fractions to indicate sale prices • Using percents to indicate test scores & probability in weather forecasts • Identifying high school math subjects • Using measurement terms to indicate height, width, depth, length, distance • Interpreting metric measurements • Identifying types of lines, geometric shapes, & solid figures • ENGLISH LANGUAGE ARTS: • Identifying types of sentences • Identifying parts of speech • Identifying punctuation marks • Providing feedback during peer-editing • Identifying steps of the writing process • Identifying types of literature • Identifying forms of writing • GEOGRAPHY: • Identifying geographical features & bodies of water • Identifying natural environments (desert, jungle, rainforest, etc.) • SCIENCE: • Identifying science classroom/laboratory equipment • Asking about equipment needed to do a science procedure • Identifying steps of the scientific method • Identifying key terms to describe the universe, solar system, & space exploration	• Telling about different types of schools in the community • Telling about schools attended, where, when, & subjects studied • Describing a school • Comparing schools in different countries • Telling about favorite school subject • Telling about extracurricular activities • Comparing extracurricular activities in different countries • Describing math education • Telling about something bought on sale • Researching & sharing information about population statistics using percents • Describing favorite books & authors • Describing newspapers & magazines read • Telling about use of different types of written communication • Describing the geography of your country • Describing geographical features experienced • Describing experience with scientific equipment • Describing science education • Brainstorming a science experiment & describing each step of the scientific method • Drawing & naming a constellation • Expressing an opinion about the importance of space exploration	0.1.2, 0.1.3, 0.1.5, 0.2.3, 1.1.2, 1.1.4, 2.5.5, 2.5.9, 2.7.5, 5.2.5, 6.0.1, 6.0.2, 6.0.4, 6.1.1, 6.1.2, 6.1.3, 6.1.4, 6.4.1, 6.4.2, 6.6.1, 6.6.2, 6.8.1	*Beg. Low:* 12, 16, 17 *Beg. High:* 7a, 12, 13, 14, 31 *Interm. Low:* 4h, 8, 9, 10, 37	LCP A: 14 LCP B: 31 LCP C: 39, 48 LCP D: 56
13 Work	• Identifying occupations • Stating work experience (including length of time in an occupation) during a job interview • Talking about occupation during social conversation • Expressing job aspirations • Identifying job skills & work activities • Indicating job skills during an interview (including length of time) • Identifying types of job advertisements (help wanted signs, job notices, classified ads) • Interpreting abbreviations in job advertisements • Identifying each step in a job-search process • Identifying workplace locations, furniture, equipment, & personnel • Identifying common office tasks • Asking the location of a co-worker • Engaging in small-talk with co-workers • Identifying common office supplies • Making requests at work • Repeating to confirm understanding of a request or instruction • Identifying factory locations, equipment, & personnel • Asking the location of workplace departments & personnel to orient oneself as a new employee • Asking about the location & activities of a co-worker • Identifying construction site machinery, equipment, and building materials • Asking a co-worker for a workplace item • Warning a co-worker of a safety hazard • Asking whether there is a sufficient supply of workplace materials • Identifying job safety equipment • Interpreting warning signs at work • Reminding someone to use safety equipment • Asking the location of emergency equipment at work	• Career exploration: sharing ideas about occupations that are interesting, difficult • Describing occupation & occupations of family members • Describing job skills • Describing a familiar job (skill requirements, qualifications, hours, salary) • Telling about how people found their jobs • Telling about experience with a job search or job interview • Describing a familiar workplace • Telling about office & school supplies used • Describing a nearby factory & working conditions there • Comparing products produced by factories in different countries • Describing building materials used in ones dwelling • Describing a nearby construction site • Telling about experience with safety equipment • Describing the use of safety equipment in the community	0.1.2, 0.1.6, 4.1.2, 4.1.3, 4.1.5, 4.1.6, 4.1.7, 4.1.8, 4.3.1, 4.3.3, 4.3.4, 4.5.1, 4.6.1, 7.1.1, 7.5.5	*Beg. Low:* 11, 12, 14, 48, 49, 50, 51, 52, 53, 54, 56 *Beg. High:* 7a, 8a, 11, 51, 54 *Interm. Low:* 1, 3, 4c, 5, 33, 34, 36	LCP A: 01, 02, 03, 04, 10 LCP B: 18, 19, 20, 21, 27 LCP C: 35, 36, 38, 44 LCP D: 52, 53, 55, 56

Unit / Theme	Communication Skills	Writing & Discussion	CASAS	LAUSD	LCPs
14 Transportation and Travel	• Identifying modes of local & inter-city public transportation • Expressing intended mode of travel • Asking about a location to obtain transportation (bus stop, bus station, train station, subway station) • Locating ticket counters, information booths, fare card machines, & information signage in transportation stations • Identifying types of vehicles • Indicating to a car salesperson need for a type of vehicle • Describing a car accident • Identifying parts of a car & maintenance items • Indicating a problem with a car • Requesting service or assistance at a service station • Identifying types of highway lanes & markings, road structures (tunnels, bridges, etc.), traffic signage, & local intersection road markings • Reporting the location of an accident • Giving & following driving directions (using prepositions of motion) • Interpreting traffic signs • Warning a driver about an upcoming sign • Interpreting compass directions • Asking for driving directions • Following instructions during a driver's test • Repeating to confirm instructions • Identifying airport locations & personnel (check-in, security, gate, baggage claim, Customs & Immigration) • Asking for location of places & personnel at an airport • Indicating loss of travel documents or other items • Identifying airplane sections, seating areas, emergency equipment, & flight personnel • Identifying steps in the process of airplane travel (actions in the security area, at the gate, boarding, & being seated) • Following instructions of airport security personnel, gate attendants, & flight crew • Identifying sections of a hotel & personnel • Asking for location of places & personnel in a hotel	• Describing mode of travel to different places in the community • Describing local public transportation • Comparing transportation in different countries • Telling about common types of vehicles in different countries • Expressing opinion about favorite type of vehicle & manufacturer • Expressing opinion about most important features to look for when making a car purchase • Describing experience with car repairs • Describing a local highway • Describing a local intersection • Telling about dangerous traffic areas where many accidents occur • Describing your route from home to school • Describing how to get to different places from home and school • Describing local traffic signs • Comparing traffic signs in different countries • Describing a familiar airport • Telling about an experience with Customs & Immigration • Describing an air travel experience • Using imagination: being an airport security officer giving passengers instructions; being a flight attendant giving passengers instructions before take-off • Describing a familiar hotel • Expressing opinion about hotel jobs that are most interesting, most difficult	0.1.2, 0.1.3, 0.1.6, 1.9.1, 1.9.2, 1.9.4, 1.9.5, 1.9.6, 1.9.7, 2.2.1, 2.2.2, 2.2.3, 2.2.4, 2.5.4, 7.2.6	*Beg. Low:* 11, 13, 23, 24, 42, 48, 49 *Beg. High:* 11, 23, 41 *Interm. Low:* 4h, 5, 15, 17, 37	*LCP A:* 09 *LCP B:* 26 *LCP C:* 43 *LCP D:* 60
15 Recreation and Entertainment	• Identifying common hobbies, crafts, & games & related materials/equipment • Describing favorite leisure activities • Purchasing craft supplies, equipment, & other products in a store • Asking for & offering a suggestion for a leisure activity • Identifying places to go for outdoor recreation, entertainment, culture, etc. • Describing past weekend activities • Describing activities planned for a future day off or weekend • Identifying features & equipment in a park & playground • Asking the location of a park feature or equipment • Warning a child to be careful on playground equipment • Identifying features of a beach, common beach items, & personnel • Identifying indoor & outdoor recreation activities & sports, & related equipment & supplies • Asking if someone remembered an item when preparing for an activity • Identifying team sports & terms for players, playing fields, & equipment • Commenting on a player's performance during a game • Indicating that you can't find an item • Asking the location of sports equipment in a store • Reminding someone of items needed for a sports activity • Identifying types of winter/water sports, recreation, & equipment • Engaging in small talk about favorite sports & recreation activities • Using the telephone to inquire whether a store sells a product • Making & responding to an invitation • Following a teacher or coach's instructions during sports practice, P.E. class, & an exercise class • Identifying types of entertainment & cultural events, & the performers • Commenting on a performance • Identifying genres of music, plays, movies, & TV programs • Expressing likes about types of entertainment • Identifying musical instruments • Complimenting someone on musical ability	• Describing a favorite hobby, craft, or game • Comparing popular games in different countries, and how to play them • Describing favorite places to go & activities there • Describing a local park & playground • Describing a favorite beach & items used there • Describing an outdoor recreation experience • Describing favorite individual sports & recreation activities • Describing favorite team sports & famous players • Comparing popular sports in different countries • Describing experience with winter or water sports & recreation • Expressing opinions about Winter Olympics sports (most exciting, most dangerous) • Describing exercise habits & routines • Using imagination: being an exercise instructor leading a class • Telling about favorite types of entertainment • Comparing types of entertainment popular in different countries • Telling about favorite performers • Telling about favorite types of music, movies, & TV programs • Describing experience with a musical instrument • Comparing typical musical instruments in different countries	0.1.2, 0.1.3, 0.1.4, 0.2.4, 1.3.7, 2.1.8, 2.6.1, 2.6.2, 2.6.3, 2.7.6, 3.5.8, 3.5.9, 7.2.6	*Beg. Low:* 12, 13, 14, 32 *Beg. High:* 7a, 9a, 9c, 10c *Interm. Low:* 3, 4e, 4h, 37	*LCP A:* 05, 06 *LCP C:* 39 *LCP D:* 56

Unit / Theme	Communication Skills	Writing & Discussion	CASAS	LAUSD	LCPs
16 Nature	• Identifying places & people on a farm • Identifying farm animals & crops • Identifying animals & pets • Identifying birds & insects • Identifying fish, sea animals, amphibians, & reptiles • Asking about the presence of wildlife in an area • Identifying trees, plants, & flowers • Identifying key parts of a tree and flower • Asking for information about trees & flowers • Warning someone about poisonous vegetation in an area • Identifying sources of energy • Describing the kind of energy used to heat homes & for cooking • Expressing an opinion about good future sources of energy • Identifying behaviors that promote conservation (recycling, conserving energy, conserving water, carpooling) • Expressing concern about environmental problems • Identifying different kinds of natural disasters	• Comparing farms in different countries • Telling about local animals, animals in a zoo, & common local birds & insects • Comparing common pets in different countries • Using imagination: what animal you would like to be, & why • Telling a popular folk tale or children's story about animals, birds, or insects • Describing fish, sea animals, & reptiles in different countries • Identifying endangered species • Expressing opinions about wildlife – most interesting, beautiful, dangerous • Describing local trees & flowers, & favorites • Comparing different cultures' use of flowers at weddings, funerals, holidays, & hospitals • Expressing an opinion about an environmental problem • Telling about how people prepare for natural disasters	0.1.2, 0.1.3, 2.7.3, 5.7.1, 5.7.2, 5.7.3, 7.2.6	Interm. Low: 4h, 37	LCP A: 13 LCP C: 47 LCP D: 64
17 U.S. Civics	• Producing correct form of identification when requested (driver's license, social security card, student I.D. card, employee I.D. badge, permanent resident card, passport, visa, work permit, birth certificate, proof of residence) • Identifying the three branches of U.S. government (legislative, executive, judicial) & their functions • Identifying senators, representatives, the president, vice-president, cabinet, Supreme Court justices, & the chief justice, & the branches of government in which they work • Identifying the key buildings in each branch of government (Capitol Building, White House, Supreme Court Building) • Identifying the Constitution as "the supreme law of the land" • Identifying the Bill of Rights • Naming freedoms guaranteed by the 1st Amendment • Identifying key amendments to the Constitution • Identifying key events in United States history • Answering history questions about events and the dates they occurred • Identifying key holidays & dates they occur • Identifying legal system & court procedures (arrest, booking, obtaining legal representation, appearing in court, standing trial, acquittal, conviction, sentencing, prison, release) • Identifying people in the criminal justice system • Engaging in small talk about a TV crime show's characters & plot • Identifying rights & responsibilities of U.S. citizens • Identifying steps in applying for citizenship	• Telling about forms of identification & when needed • Describing how people in a community "exercise their 1st Amendment rights" • Brainstorming ideas for a new amendment to the Constitution • Expressing an opinion about the most important event in United States history • Telling about important events in the history of different countries • Describing U.S. holidays you celebrate • Describing holidays celebrated in different countries • Describing the legal system in different countries • Telling about an episode of a TV crime show • Expressing an opinion about the most important rights & responsibilities of people in their communities • Expressing an opinion about the rights of citizens vs. non-citizens	0.1.2, 0.1.3, 2.7.1, 2.7.3, 5.1.6, 5.2.1, 5.2.2, 5.3.3, 5.3.6, 5.3.7, 5.3.8, 5.5.2, 5.5.3, 5.5.4, 5.6.3	Beg. Low: 40 Beg. High: 40, 42 Interm. Low: 4h, 24, 25, 37	LCP A: 12 LCP B: 26, 29 LCP C: 43, 46 LCP D: 60, 63

Welcome to the second edition of the WORD BY WORD Picture Dictionary! This text presents more than 4,000 vocabulary words through vibrant illustrations and simple accessible lesson pages that are designed for clarity and ease-of-use with learners at all levels. Our goal is to prepare students for success using English in everyday life, in the community, in school, and at work. We are delighted to now include as bonus material the WordSongs Music CD, offering students entertaining musical practice to extend learning outside the classroom.

WORD BY WORD organizes the vocabulary into 17 thematic units, providing a careful research-based sequence of lessons that integrates students' development of grammar and vocabulary skills through topics that begin with the immediate world of the student and progress to the world at large. Early lessons on the family, the home, and daily activities lead to lessons on the community, school, workplace, shopping, recreation, and other topics. The text offers extensive coverage of important lifeskill competencies and the vocabulary of school subjects and extracurricular activities, and it is designed to meet the objectives of current national, state, and local standards-based curricula you can find in the Scope & Sequence on the previous pages.

Since each lesson in *Word by Word* is self-contained, it can be used either sequentially or in any desired order. For users' convenience, the lessons are listed in two ways: sequentially in the Table of Contents, and alphabetically in the Thematic Index. These resources, combined with the Glossary in the appendix, allow students and teachers to quickly and easily locate all words and topics in the Picture Dictionary.

The *Word by Word* Picture Dictionary is the centerpiece of the complete *Word by Word* Vocabulary Development Program, which offers a wide selection of print and media support materials for instruction at all levels.

A unique choice of workbooks at Beginning and Intermediate levels offers flexible options to meet students' needs. Vocabulary Workbooks feature motivating vocabulary, grammar, and listening practice, and standards-based Lifeskills Workbooks provide competency-based activities and reading tied to national, state, and local curriculum frameworks. A Literacy Workbook is also available.

The Teacher's Guide and Lesson Planner with CD-ROM includes lesson-planning suggestions, community tasks, Internet weblinks, and reproducible masters to save teachers hours of lesson preparation time. An Activity Handbook with step-by-step teaching strategies for key vocabulary development activities is included in the Teacher's Guide.

The Music CD included with this student book contains vocal versions of all the WordSongs. The separate Audio Program includes all words and conversations in the student book for interactive practice, plus both vocal and sing-along versions of all the WordSongs for entertaining classroom practice through music.

Additional ancillary materials include Color Transparencies, Vocabulary Game Cards, and a Testing Program. Bilingual Editions are also available.

Teaching Strategies

Word by Word presents vocabulary words in context. Model conversations depict situations in which people use the words in meaningful communication. These models become the basis for students to engage in dynamic, interactive practice. In addition, writing and discussion questions in each lesson encourage students to relate the vocabulary and themes to their own lives as they share experiences, thoughts, opinions, and information about themselves, their cultures, and their countries. In this way, students get to know each other "word by word."

In using *Word by Word*, we encourage you to develop approaches and strategies that are compatible with your own teaching style and the needs and abilities of your students. You may find it helpful to incorporate some of the following techniques for presenting and practicing the vocabulary in each lesson.

1. **Preview the Vocabulary:** Activate students' prior knowledge of the vocabulary by brainstorming with students the words in the lesson they already know and writing them on the board, or by having students look at the transparency or the illustration in *Word by Word* and identify the words they are familiar with.

2. **Present the Vocabulary:** Using the transparency or the illustration in the Picture Dictionary, point to the picture of each word, say the word, and have the class repeat it chorally and individually. (You can also play the word list on the Audio Program.) Check students' understanding and pronunciation of the vocabulary.

3. **Vocabulary Practice:** Have students practice the vocabulary as a class, in pairs, or in small groups. Say or write a word, and have students point to the item or tell the number. Or, point to an item or give the number, and have students say the word.

4. **Model Conversation Practice:** Some lessons have model conversations that use the first word in the vocabulary list. Other models are in the form of skeletal dialogs, in which vocabulary words can be inserted. (In many skeletal dialogs, bracketed numbers indicate which words can be used for practicing the conversation. If no bracketed numbers appear, all the words in the lesson can be used.)

   The following steps are recommended for Model Conversation Practice:

   a. Preview: Have students look at the model illustration and discuss who they think the speakers are and where the conversation takes place.

   b. The teacher presents the model or plays the audio one or more times and checks students' understanding of the situation and the vocabulary.

   c. Students repeat each line of the conversation chorally and individually.

   d. Students practice the model in pairs.

   e. A pair of students presents a conversation based on the model, but using a different word from the vocabulary list.

   f. In pairs, students practice several conversations based on the model, using different words on the page.

   g. Pairs present their conversations to the class.

5. **Additional Conversation Practice:** Many lessons provide two additional skeletal dialogs for further conversation practice with the vocabulary. (These can be found in the yellow-shaded area at the bottom of the page.) Have students practice and present these conversations using any words they wish. Before they practice the additional conversations, you may want to have students listen to the sample additional conversations on the Audio Program.

6. **Spelling Practice:** Have students practice spelling the words as a class, in pairs, or in small groups. Say a word, and have students spell it aloud or write it. Or, using the transparency, point to an item and have students write the word.

7. **Themes for Discussion, Composition, Journals, and Portfolios:** Each lesson of *Word by Word* provides one or more questions for discussion and composition. (These can be found in a blue-shaded area at the bottom of the page.) Have students respond to the questions as a class, in pairs, or in small groups. Or, have students write their responses at home, share their written work with other students, and discuss as a class, in pairs, or in small groups.

   Students may enjoy keeping a journal of their written work. If time permits, you may want to write a response in each student's journal, sharing your own opinions and experiences as well as reacting to what the student has written. If you are keeping portfolios of students' work, these compositions serve as excellent examples of students' progress in learning English.

8. **Communication Activities:** The *Word by Word* Teacher's Guide and Lesson Planner with CD-ROM provides a wealth of games, tasks, brainstorming, discussion, movement, drawing, miming, role-playing, and other activities designed to take advantage of students' different learning styles and particular abilities and strengths. For each lesson, choose one or more of these activities to reinforce students' vocabulary learning in a way that is stimulating, creative, and enjoyable.

   WORD BY WORD aims to offer students a communicative, meaningful, and lively way of practicing English vocabulary. In conveying to you the substance of our program, we hope that we have also conveyed the spirit: that learning vocabulary can be genuinely interactive . . . relevant to our students' lives . . . responsive to students' differing strengths and learning styles . . . and fun!

   Steven J. Molinsky

   Bill Bliss

Registration Form

Name	Gloria	P.	Sanchez
	First	Middle Initial	Last

Address	95	Garden Street	3G
	Number	Street	Apartment Number
	Los Angeles	CA	90036
	City	State	Zip Code

Telephone ___323-524-3278___   Cell Phone ___323-695-1864___

E-Mail Address ___gloria97@ail.com___   SSN ___227-93-6185___   Sex M__ F **X**

Date of Birth ___5/12/88___   Place of Birth ___Centerville, Texas___

1 name	**6** street number	**12** area code	**17** sex
2 first name	**7** street	**13** telephone number / phone number	**18** date of birth
3 middle initial	**8** apartment number	**14** cell phone number	**19** place of birth
4 last name / family name / surname	**9** city	**15** e-mail address	
5 address	**10** state	**16** social security number	
	11 zip code		

A. What's your **name**?
B. Gloria P. Sanchez.

A. What's your _____?
B. ....
A. Did you say ....?
B. Yes. That's right.

A. What's your last name?
B. ....
A. How do you spell that?
B. ....

Tell about yourself:
    My name is ....
    My address is ....
    My telephone number is ....

Now interview a friend.

1 husband	**children**	**siblings**	**grandparents**	**grandchildren**
2 wife	**5** daughter	**8** sister	**10** grandmother	**12** granddaughter
	6 son	**9** brother	**11** grandfather	**13** grandson
parents	**7** baby			
3 father				
4 mother				

A. Who is he?
B. He's my **husband**.
A. What's his name?
B. His name is *Jack*.

A. Who is she?
B. She's my **wife**.
A. What's her name?
B. Her name is *Nancy*.

A. I'd like to introduce my _____.
B. Nice to meet you.
C. Nice to meet you, too.

A. What's your _____'s name?
B. His/Her name is ....

Who are the people in your family?
What are their names?

Tell about photos of family members.

Helen

Walter

Jack

Nancy

Frank

Linda

Jennifer

Timmy

Alan

1 uncle	**6**	mother-in-law
2 aunt	**7**	father-in-law
3 niece	**8**	son-in-law
4 nephew	**9**	daughter-in-law
5 cousin	**10**	brother-in-law
	11	sister-in-law

① Jack is Alan's ___.
② Nancy is Alan's ___.
③ Jennifer is Frank and Linda's ___.
④ Timmy is Frank and Linda's ___.
⑤ Alan is Jennifer and Timmy's ___.

⑥ Helen is Jack's ___.
⑦ Walter is Jack's ___.
⑧ Jack is Helen and Walter's ___.
⑨ Linda is Helen and Walter's ___.
⑩ Frank is Jack's ___.
⑪ Linda is Jack's ___.

A. Who is he/she?
B. He's/She's my _____.
A. What's his/her name?
B. His/Her name is _____.

A. Let me introduce my _____.
B. I'm glad to meet you.
C. Nice meeting you, too.

Tell about your relatives:
What are their names?
Where do they live?

Draw your family tree and tell about it.

1 teacher	**6** table	**11** clock	**15** whiteboard / board
2 teacher's aide	**7** computer	**12** map	**16** globe
3 student	**8** overhead projector	**13** bulletin board	**17** bookcase/bookshelf
4 desk	**9** screen	**14** P.A. system / loudspeaker	**18** teacher's desk
5 seat / chair	**10** chalkboard / board		**19** wastebasket

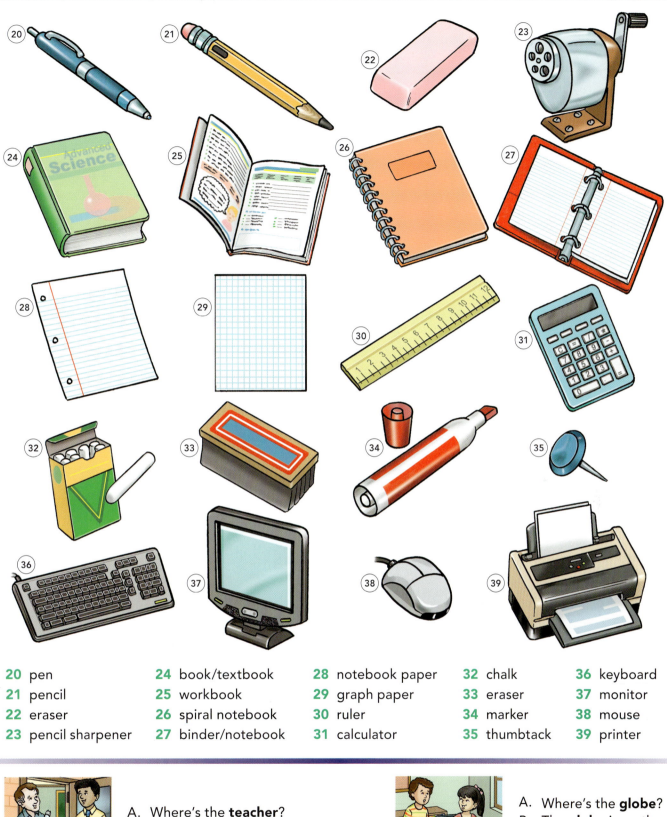

20 pen	**24** book/textbook	**28** notebook paper	**32** chalk	**36** keyboard
21 pencil	**25** workbook	**29** graph paper	**33** eraser	**37** monitor
22 eraser	**26** spiral notebook	**30** ruler	**34** marker	**38** mouse
23 pencil sharpener	**27** binder/notebook	**31** calculator	**35** thumbtack	**39** printer

A. Where's the **teacher**?
B. The **teacher** is *next to* the **board**.

A. Where's the **globe**?
B. The **globe** is *on* the **bookcase**.

A. Is there a/an _____ in your classroom?*
B. Yes. There's a/an _____
   next to/on the _____.

A. Is there a/an _____ in your classroom?*
B. No, there isn't.

Describe your classroom.
(There's a/an ....)

* *With 28, 29, 32 use:* Is there _____ in your classroom?

1 Say your name.
2 Repeat your name.
3 Spell your name.
4 Print your name.
5 Sign your name.

6 Stand up.
7 Go to the board.
8 Write on the board.
9 Erase the board.
10 Sit down. / Take your seat.

11 Open your book.
12 Read page ten.
13 Study page ten.
14 Close your book.
15 Put away your book.

16 Raise your hand.
17 Ask a question.
18 Listen to the question.
19 Answer the question.
20 Listen to the answer.

21 Do your homework.
22 Bring in your homework.
23 Go over the answers.
24 Correct your mistakes.
25 Hand in your homework.

26 Share a book.
27 Discuss the question.
28 Help each other.
29 Work together.
30 Share with the class.

31 Look in the dictionary.
32 Look up a word.
33 Pronounce the word.
34 Read the definition.
35 Copy the word.

36 Work alone./Do your own work.
37 Work with a partner.
38 Break up into small groups.
39 Work in a group.
40 Work as a class.

41 Lower the shades.
42 Turn off the lights.
43 Look at the screen.
44 Take notes.
45 Turn on the lights.

46 Take out a piece of paper.
47 Pass out the tests.
48 Answer the questions.
49 Check your answers.
50 Collect the tests.

51 Choose the correct answer.
52 Circle the correct answer.
53 Fill in the blank.
54 Mark the answer sheet. / Bubble the answer.
55 Match the words.

56 Underline the word.
57 Cross out the word.
58 Unscramble the word.
59 Put the words in order.
60 Write on a separate sheet of paper.

You're the teacher!
Give instructions to your students!

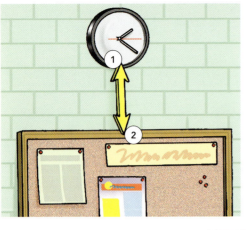

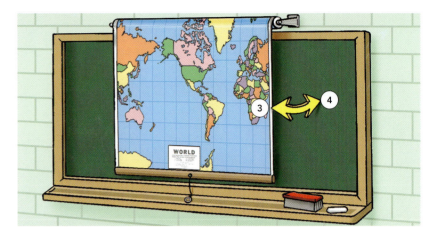

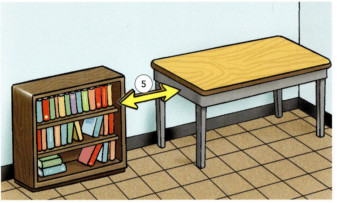

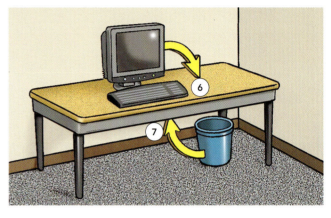

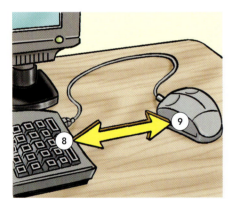

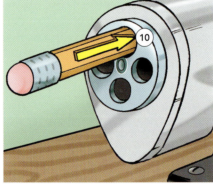

1 above

2 below

3 in front of

4 behind

5 next to

6 on

7 under

8 to the left of

9 to the right of

10 in

11 between

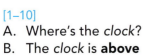

[1–10]

A. Where's the *clock*?

B. The *clock* is **above** the *bulletin board*.

[11]

A. Where's the *dictionary*?

B. The *dictionary* is **between** the *globe* and the *pencil sharpener*.

Tell about the classroom on page 4. Use the prepositions in this lesson.

Tell about your classroom.

1 get up
2 take a shower
3 brush *my** teeth
4 shave
5 get dressed

6 wash *my** face
7 put on makeup
8 brush *my** hair
9 comb *my** hair
10 make the bed

11 get undressed
12 take a bath
13 go to bed
14 sleep

15 make breakfast
16 make lunch
17 cook / make dinner
18 eat / have breakfast
19 eat / have lunch
20 eat / have dinner

* my, his, her, our, your, their

A. What do you do every day?
B. **I get up, I take a shower**, and **I brush my teeth**.

A. What does he do every day?
B. He _____ s, he _____ s, and he _____ s.

A. What does she do every day?
B. She _____ s, she _____ s, and she _____ s.

What do you do every day? Make a list.

Interview some friends and tell about their everyday activities.

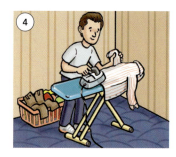

1 clean the apartment / clean the house
2 wash the dishes
3 do the laundry
4 iron

5 feed the baby
6 feed the cat
7 walk the dog
8 study

9 go to work
10 go to school
11 drive to work
12 take the bus to school

13 work
14 leave work
15 go to the store
16 come home / get home

A. Hello. What are you doing?
B. I'm **clean**ing the **apartment**.

A. Hello, ... This is ....
   What are you doing?
B. I'm _____ing. How about you?
A. I'm _____ing.

A. Are you going to _____ soon?
B. Yes. I'm going to _____ in a
   little while.

What are you going to do tomorrow?
Make a list of everything you are
going to do.

1 watch TV
2 listen to the radio
3 listen to music
4 read a book

5 read the newspaper
6 play
7 play cards
8 play basketball

9 play the guitar
10 practice the piano
11 exercise
12 swim

13 plant flowers
14 use the computer
15 write a letter
16 relax

A. Hi. What are you doing?
B. I'm **watch**ing **TV**.

A. Hi, ... Are you
   _____ing?
B. No, I'm not. I'm _____ing.

A. What's your (husband/wife/son/
   daughter/. . .) doing?
B. He's/She's _____ing.

What leisure activities do you like to do?

What do your family members and
friends like to do?

Greeting People

Leave Taking

1 Hello. / Hi.
2 Good morning.
3 Good afternoon.
4 Good evening.

5 How are you? / How are you doing?
6 Fine. / Fine, thanks. / Okay.
7 What's new? / What's new with you?
8 Not much. / Not too much.

9 Good-bye. / Bye.
10 Good night.
11 See you later. / See you soon.

Introducing Yourself and Others

Getting Someone's Attention

Expressing Gratitude

Saying You Don't Understand

Calling Someone on the Telephone

12 Hello. My name is ..../
   Hi. I'm ....
13 Nice to meet you.
14 Nice to meet you, too.
15 I'd like to introduce ..../
   This is ....

16 Excuse me.
17 May I ask a question?
18 Thank you. / Thanks.
19 You're welcome.

20 I don't understand. /
   Sorry. I don't understand.
21 Can you please repeat that? /
   Can you please say that again?
22 Hello. This is .... May I please
   speak to ....?
23 Yes. Hold on a moment.
24 I'm sorry. .... isn't here right now.

Practice conversations with other students. Use all the expressions on pages 12 and 13.

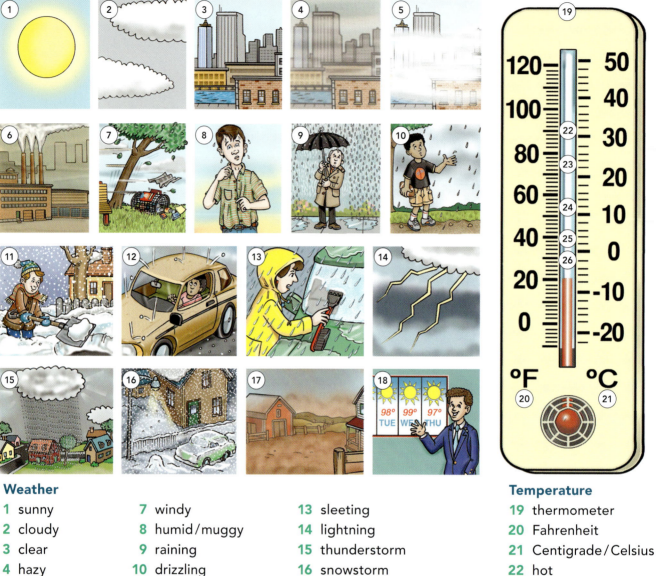

Weather

1 sunny
2 cloudy
3 clear
4 hazy
5 foggy
6 smoggy

7 windy
8 humid / muggy
9 raining
10 drizzling
11 snowing
12 hailing

13 sleeting
14 lightning
15 thunderstorm
16 snowstorm
17 dust storm
18 heat wave

Temperature

19 thermometer
20 Fahrenheit
21 Centigrade / Celsius
22 hot
23 warm
24 cool
25 cold
26 freezing

[1–13]
A. What's the weather like?
B. It's _____.

[14–18]
A. What's the weather forecast?
B. There's going to be ___[14]___ /
   a ___[15–18]___.

[20–26]
A. How's the weather?
B. It's ___[22–26]___.
A. What's the temperature?
B. It's . . . degrees ___[20–21]___.

What's the weather like today? What's the temperature?

What's the weather forecast for tomorrow?

Cardinal Numbers

0 zero	**11** eleven	**21** twenty-one	**101** one hundred (and) one
1 one	**12** twelve	**22** twenty-two	**102** one hundred (and) two
2 two	**13** thirteen	**30** thirty	**1,000** one thousand
3 three	**14** fourteen	**40** forty	**10,000** ten thousand
4 four	**15** fifteen	**50** fifty	**100,000** one hundred thousand
5 five	**16** sixteen	**60** sixty	**1,000,000** one million
6 six	**17** seventeen	**70** seventy	**1,000,000,000** one billion
7 seven	**18** eighteen	**80** eighty	
8 eight	**19** nineteen	**90** ninety	
9 nine	**20** twenty	**100** one hundred	
10 ten			

A. How old are you?
B. I'm _____ years old.

A. How many people are there in your family?
B. _____.

Ordinal Numbers

1st first	**11th** eleventh	**21st** twenty-first	**101st** one hundred (and) first
2nd second	**12th** twelfth	**22nd** twenty-second	**102nd** one hundred (and) second
3rd third	**13th** thirteenth	**30th** thirtieth	**1,000th** one thousandth
4th fourth	**14th** fourteenth	**40th** fortieth	**10,000th** ten thousandth
5th fifth	**15th** fifteenth	**50th** fiftieth	**100,000th** one hundred thousandth
6th sixth	**16th** sixteenth	**60th** sixtieth	**1,000,000th** one millionth
7th seventh	**17th** seventeenth	**70th** seventieth	**1,000,000,000th** one billionth
8th eighth	**18th** eighteenth	**80th** eightieth	
9th ninth	**19th** nineteenth	**90th** ninetieth	
10th tenth	**20th** twentieth	**100th** one hundredth	

A. What floor do you live on?
B. I live on the _____ floor.

A. Is this your first trip to our country?
B. No. It's my _____ trip.

How many students are there in your class?

How many people are there in your country?

What were the names of your teachers in elementary school? (My *first*-grade teacher was Ms./Mrs./Mr. . . .)

| *two* o'clock | *two* fifteen / a quarter after *two* | *two* thirty / half past *two* | *two* forty-five / a quarter to *three* |

| *two* oh five | *two* twenty / twenty after *two* | *two* forty / twenty to *three* | *two* fifty-five / five to *three* |

A. What time is it?
B. It's _____.

A. What time does the movie begin?
B. At _____.

| *two* A.M. | *two* P.M. | noon / twelve noon | midnight / twelve midnight |

A. When does the train leave?
B. At _____.

A. What time will we arrive?
B. At _____.

Tell about your daily schedule:
    What do you do? When?
    (I get up at _____. I ....)

Do you usually have enough time to do things, or do you "run out of time"? Tell about it.

Tell about the use of time in different cultures or countries you know:
    Do people arrive on time for work? appointments? parties?
    Do trains and buses operate exactly on schedule?
    Do movies and sports events begin on time?
    Do workplaces use time clocks or timesheets to record employees' work hours?

Coins

Name	Value	Written as:	
1 penny	one cent	1¢	$ .01
2 nickel	five cents	5¢	$ .05
3 dime	ten cents	10¢	$ .10
4 quarter	twenty-five cents	25¢	$ .25
5 half dollar	fifty cents	50¢	$ .50
6 silver dollar	one dollar		$1.00

A. How much is a **penny** worth?

B. A **penny** is worth **one cent**.

A. *Soda* costs *ninety-five cents.* Do you have enough change?

B. Yes. I have a/two/three _____(s) and . . . .

Currency

Name	We sometimes say:	Value	Written as:
7 (one-) dollar bill	a one	one dollar	$ 1.00
8 five-dollar bill	a five	five dollars	$ 5.00
9 ten-dollar bill	a ten	ten dollars	$ 10.00
10 twenty-dollar bill	a twenty	twenty dollars	$ 20.00
11 fifty-dollar bill	a fifty	fifty dollars	$ 50.00
12 (one-) hundred dollar bill	a hundred	one hundred dollars	$100.00

A. I'm going to the supermarket. Do you have any cash?

B. I have a **twenty-dollar bill**.

A. **Twenty dollars** is enough. Thanks.

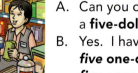

A. Can you change a **five-dollar bill**/a **five**?

B. Yes. I have *five one-dollar bills*/*five ones.*

Written as:	We say:
$1.30	a dollar and thirty cents a dollar thirty
$2.50	two dollars and fifty cents two fifty
$56.49	fifty-six dollars and forty-nine cents fifty-six forty-nine

Tell about some things you usually buy. What do they cost?

Name and describe the coins and currency in your country. What are they worth in U.S. dollars?

Days of the Week

1 year
2 month
3 week
4 day
5 weekend

6 Sunday
7 Monday
8 Tuesday
9 Wednesday
10 Thursday
11 Friday
12 Saturday

Months of the Year

13 January
14 February
15 March
16 April
17 May
18 June

19 July
20 August
21 September
22 October
23 November
24 December

25 January 3, 2012
    January third, two
      thousand twelve
26 birthday
27 anniversary
28 appointment

A. What year is it?
B. It's _____.

[13–24]
A. What month is it?
B. It's _____.

[6–12]
A. What day is it?
B. It's _____.

A. What's today's date?
B. It's _____.

[26–28]
A. When is your _____?
B. It's on _____.

Which days of the week do you
go to work/school?
(I go to work/school on _____.)

What do you do on the weekend?

What is your date of birth?
(I was born on ....._month day year_.....)

What's your favorite day of the week?
Why?

What's your favorite month of the
year? Why?

1 yesterday
2 today
3 tomorrow

4 morning
5 afternoon
6 evening
7 night

8 yesterday morning
9 yesterday afternoon
10 yesterday evening
11 last night

12 this morning
13 this afternoon
14 this evening
15 tonight

16 tomorrow morning
17 tomorrow afternoon
18 tomorrow evening
19 tomorrow night

20 last week
21 this week
22 next week

23 once a week
24 twice a week
25 three times a week
26 every day

Seasons
27 spring
28 summer
29 fall / autumn
30 winter

What did you do yesterday morning / afternoon / evening?

What did you do last night?

What are you going to do tomorrow morning / afternoon / evening / night?

What did you do last week?

What are your plans for next week?

How many times a week do you have English class? / go to the supermarket? / exercise?

What's your favorite season? Why?

1 apartment building	**5** condominium/condo	**9** shelter	**13** the city
2 house	**6** dormitory/dorm	**10** farm	**14** the suburbs
3 duplex/two-family house	**7** mobile home	**11** ranch	**15** the country
4 townhouse/townhome	**8** nursing home	**12** houseboat	**16** a town/village

A. Where do you live?

B. I live { in a/an _____ [1–9].
on a _____ [10–12].
in _____ [13–16].

[1–12]

A. Town Taxi Company.
B. Hello. Please send a taxi to
....*(address)*....
A. Is that a house or an
apartment building?
B. It's a/an _____.
A. All right. We'll be there
right away.

[1–12]

A. This is the Emergency Operator.
B. Please send an ambulance to
....*(address)*....
A. Is that a private home?
B. It's a/an _____.
A. What's your name and telephone number?
B. ....

Tell about people you know and where they live.

Discuss:
Who lives in dormitories?
Who lives in nursing homes?
Who lives in shelters?
Why?

1 bookcase	**9** VCR/video cassette recorder	**16** speaker	**24** lamp
2 picture/photograph		**17** stereo system	**25** lampshade
3 painting	**10** wall	**18** magazine holder	**26** end table
4 mantel	**11** ceiling	**19** (throw) pillow	**27** floor
5 fireplace	**12** drapes	**20** sofa/couch	**28** floor lamp
6 fireplace screen	**13** window	**21** plant	**29** armchair
7 DVD player	**14** loveseat	**22** coffee table	
8 television/TV	**15** wall unit	**23** rug	

A. Where are you?
B. I'm in the living room.
A. What are you doing?
B. I'm dusting* the **bookcase**.

* dusting/cleaning

A. You have a very nice living room!
B. Thank you.
A. Your _____ is/are beautiful!
B. Thank you for saying so.

A. Uh-oh! I just spilled coffee on your _____!
B. That's okay. Don't worry about it.

Tell about your living room.
(In my living room there's ....)

1 (dining room) table	**10** chandelier	**19** platter	**27** knife
2 (dining room) chair	**11** china cabinet	**20** butter dish	**28** spoon
3 buffet	**12** china	**21** salt shaker	**29** bowl
4 tray	**13** salad bowl	**22** pepper shaker	**30** mug
5 teapot	**14** serving bowl	**23** tablecloth	**31** glass
6 coffee pot	**15** serving dish	**24** napkin	**32** cup
7 sugar bowl	**16** vase	**25** fork	**33** saucer
8 creamer	**17** candle	**26** plate	
9 pitcher	**18** candlestick		

A. This **dining room table** is very nice.
B. Thank you. It was a gift from my *grandmother*.*

*grandmother/grandfather/aunt/uncle/. . .

[In a store]
A. May I help you?
B. Yes, please. Do you have _____s?*
A.   Yes. _____s* are right over there.
B. Thank you.

*With 12, use the singular.

[At home]
A. Look at this old _____ I just bought!
B. Where did you buy it?
A. At a yard sale. How do you like it?
B. It's VERY unusual!

Tell about your dining room.
(In my dining room there's
..............)

1 bed	8 electric blanket	15 curtains	21 jewelry box
2 headboard	9 dust ruffle	16 lamp	22 dresser/bureau
3 pillow	10 bedspread	17 alarm clock	23 mattress
4 pillowcase	11 comforter/quilt	18 clock radio	24 box spring
5 fitted sheet	12 carpet	19 night table/nightstand	25 bed frame
6 (flat) sheet	13 chest (of drawers)	20 mirror	
7 blanket	14 blinds		

A. Ooh! Look at that big bug!
B. Where?
A. It's on the **bed**!
B. I'LL get it.

[In a store]
A. Excuse me. I'm looking for a/an _____.*
B. We have some very nice _____s, and they're all on sale this week!
A. Oh, good!

[In a bedroom]
A. Oh, no! I just lost my contact lens!
B. Where?
A. I think it's on the _____.
B. I'll help you look.

Tell about your bedroom.
(In my bedroom there's ....)

* With 14 & 15, use: Excuse me. I'm looking for _____.

1 refrigerator	10 dishwashing liquid	19 blender	28 coffeemaker
2 freezer	11 faucet	20 toaster oven	29 trash compactor
3 garbage pail	12 (kitchen) sink	21 microwave (oven)	30 cutting board
4 (electric) mixer	13 dishwasher	22 potholder	31 cookbook
5 cabinet	14 (garbage) disposal	23 tea kettle	32 food processor
6 paper towel holder	15 dish towel	24 stove/range	33 kitchen chair
7 canister	16 dish rack/dish drainer	25 burner	34 kitchen table
8 (kitchen) counter	17 spice rack	26 oven	35 placemat
9 dishwasher detergent	18 (electric) can opener	27 toaster	

A. I think we need a new **refrigerator**.
B. I think you're right.

[In a store]
A. Excuse me. Are your _____s still on sale?
B. Yes, they are. They're twenty percent off.

[In a kitchen]
A. When did you get this/these new _____(s)?
B. I got it/them last week.

Tell about your kitchen.
(In my kitchen there's ....)

1 teddy bear	**9** changing pad	**17** rattle	**25** booster seat
2 baby monitor/intercom	**10** diaper pail	**18** walker	**26** baby seat
3 chest (of drawers)	**11** night light	**19** cradle	**27** high chair
4 crib	**12** toy chest	**20** stroller	**28** portable crib
5 crib bumper/bumper pad	**13** stuffed animal	**21** baby carriage	**29** potty
6 mobile	**14** doll	**22** car seat/safety seat	**30** baby frontpack
7 changing table	**15** swing	**23** baby carrier	**31** baby backpack
8 stretch suit	**16** playpen	**24** food warmer	

A. Thank you for the **teddy bear**. It's a very nice gift.
B. You're welcome. Tell me, when are you due?
A. In a few more weeks.

A. That's a very nice _____.
   Where did you get it?
B. It was a gift from ....

A. Do you have everything you need
   before the baby comes?
B. Almost everything. We're still
   looking for a/an _____ and a/an
   _____.

Tell about your country:
   What things do people buy for a new baby?
   Does a new baby sleep in a separate room,
   as in the United States?

1 wastebasket	10 cup	19 hand towel	28 shower
2 vanity	11 toothbrush	20 washcloth/facecloth	29 shower head
3 soap	12 toothbrush holder	21 towel rack	30 shower curtain
4 soap dish	13 electric toothbrush	22 plunger	31 bathtub/tub
5 soap dispenser	14 hair dryer	23 toilet brush	32 rubber mat
6 (bathroom) sink	15 shelf	24 toilet paper	33 drain
7 faucet	16 hamper	25 air freshener	34 sponge
8 medicine cabinet	17 fan	26 toilet	35 bath mat
9 mirror	18 bath towel	27 toilet seat	36 scale

A. Where's the **hair dryer**?
B. It's *on* the **vanity**.

A. Where's the **soap**?
B. It's *in* the **soap dish**.

A. Where's the **plunger**?
B. It's *next to* the **toilet brush**.

A. [Knock. Knock.] Did I leave my glasses in there?
B. Yes. They're on/in/next to the _____.

A. *Bobby*? You didn't clean up the bathroom! There's toothpaste on the _____, and there's powder all over the _____!
B. Sorry. I'll clean it up right away.

Tell about your bathroom.
(In my bathroom there's ....)

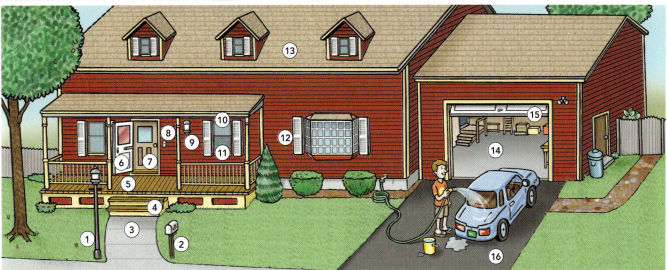

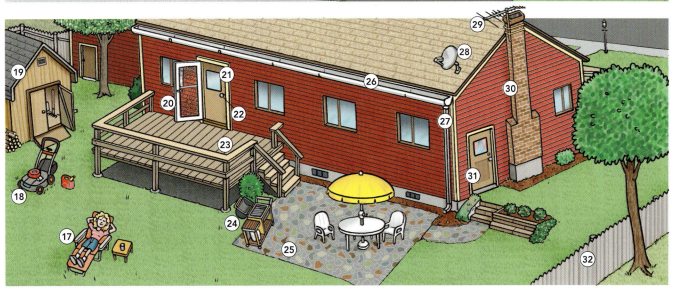

Front Yard

1	lamppost	9	(front) light
2	mailbox	10	window
3	front walk	11	(window) screen
4	front steps	12	shutter
5	(front) porch	13	roof
6	storm door	14	garage
7	front door	15	garage door
8	doorbell	16	driveway

Backyard

17	lawn chair	25	patio
18	lawnmower	26	gutter
19	tool shed	27	drainpipe
20	screen door	28	satellite dish
21	back door	29	TV antenna
22	door knob	30	chimney
23	deck	31	side door
24	barbecue/(outdoor) grill	32	fence

A. When are you going to repair the **lamppost**?
B. I'm going to repair it next Saturday.

[On the telephone]
A. Harry's Home Repairs.
B. Hello. Do you fix _____s?
A. No, we don't.
B. Oh, okay. Thank you.

[At work on Monday morning]
A. What did you do this weekend?
B. Nothing much. I repaired my
_____ and my _____.

Do you like to repair things?
What things can you repair yourself?
What things can't you repair? Who
repairs them?

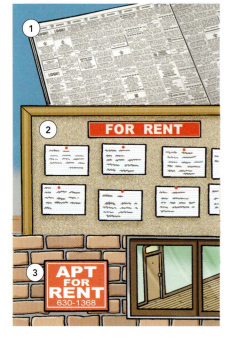

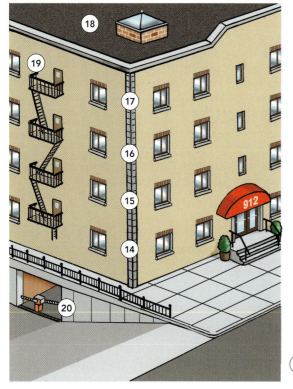

Looking for an Apartment
1 apartment ads / classified ads
2 apartment listings
3 vacancy sign

Signing a Lease
4 tenant
5 landlord
6 lease
7 security deposit

Moving In
8 moving truck / moving van
9 neighbor
10 building manager
11 doorman
12 key
13 lock

14 first floor
15 second floor
16 third floor
17 fourth floor
18 roof
19 fire escape
20 parking garage

21 balcony
22 courtyard
23 parking lot
24 parking space
25 swimming pool
26 whirlpool
27 trash bin
28 air conditioner

Lobby
29 intercom/speaker
30 buzzer
31 mailbox
32 elevator
33 stairway

Doorway
34 peephole
35 (door) chain
36 dead-bolt lock
37 smoke detector

Hallway
38 fire exit/
emergency stairway
39 fire alarm
40 sprinkler system
41 superintendent
42 garbage chute/
trash chute

Basement
43 storage room
44 storage locker
45 laundry room
46 security gate

[19–46]
A. Is there a **fire escape**?
B. Yes, there is. Do you want to see the apartment?
A. Yes, I do.

[19–46]
　　[Renting an apartment]
A. Let me show you around.
B. Okay.
A. This is the _____, and
here's the _____.
B. I see.

[19–46]
　　[On the telephone]
A. Mom and Dad? I found an apartment.
B. Good. Tell us about it.
A. It has a/an _____ and a/an _____.
B. That's nice. Does it have a/an _____?
A. Yes, it does.

Do you or someone you know live in an
apartment building? Tell about it.

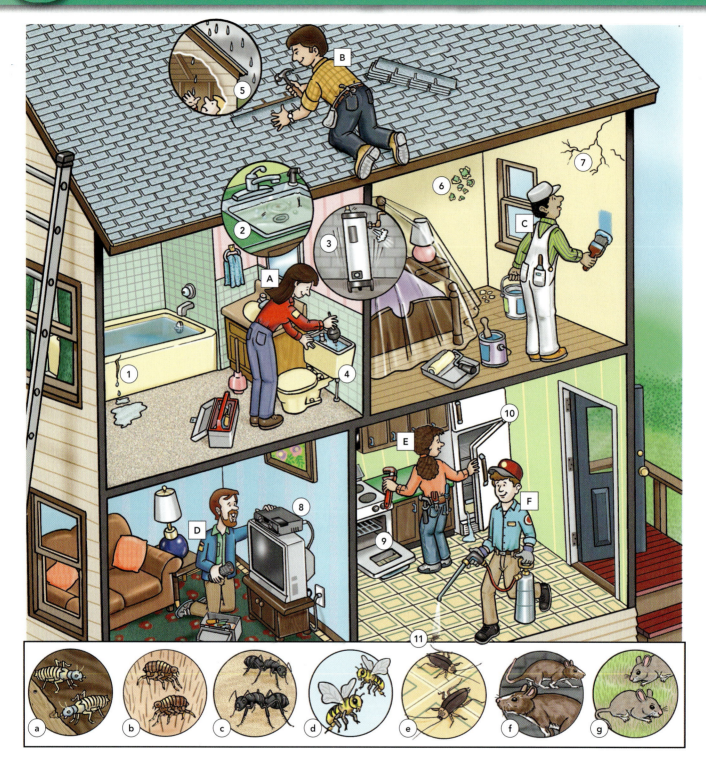

A plumber
1 The bathtub is leaking.
2 The sink is clogged.
3 The hot water heater isn't working.
4 The toilet is broken.

B roofer
5 The roof is leaking.

C (house) painter
6 The paint is peeling.
7 The wall is cracked.

D cable TV company
8 The cable TV isn't working.

E appliance repairperson
9 The stove isn't working.
10 The refrigerator is broken.

**F exterminator/
pest control specialist**
11 There are _____ in the kitchen.
  a termites
  b fleas
  c ants
  d bees
  e cockroaches
  f rats
  g mice

G locksmith
12 The lock is broken.

H electrician
13 The front light doesn't go on.
14 The doorbell doesn't ring.
15 The power is out in the living room.

I chimneysweep
16 The chimney is dirty.

J home repairperson/ "handyman"
17 The tiles in the bathroom are loose.

K carpenter
18 The steps are broken.
19 The door doesn't open.

L heating and air conditioning service
20 The heating system is broken.
21 The air conditioning isn't working.

A. What's the matter?
B. ___[1–21]___.
A. I think we should call a/an ___[A–L]___.

[1–21]
A. I'm having a problem in my apartment/house.
B. What's the problem?
A. _____.

[A–L]
A. Can you recommend a good _____?
B. Yes. You should call ....

What do you do when there are problems in your home? Do you fix things yourself, or do you call someone?

A sweep the floor
B vacuum
C mop the floor
D wash the windows
E dust
F wax the floor
G polish the furniture
H clean the bathroom
I take out the garbage

1 broom
2 dustpan
3 whisk broom
4 carpet sweeper
5 vacuum (cleaner)
6 vacuum cleaner attachments
7 vacuum cleaner bag
8 hand vacuum

9 (dust) mop/ (dry) mop
10 (sponge) mop
11 (wet) mop
12 paper towels
13 window cleaner
14 ammonia
15 dust cloth
16 feather duster

17 floor wax
18 furniture polish
19 cleanser
20 scrub brush
21 sponge
22 bucket/pail
23 trash can/ garbage can
24 recycling bin

[A–I]
A. What are you doing?
B. I'm **sweep**ing **the floor**.

[1–24]
A. I can't find the **broom**.
B. Look over there!

[1–12, 15, 16, 20–24]
A. Excuse me. Do you sell _____(s)?
B. Yes. They're at the back of the store.
A. Thanks.

[13, 14, 17–19]
A. Excuse me. Do you sell _____?
B. Yes. It's at the back of the store.
A. Thanks.

What household cleaning chores do people do in your home? What things do they use?

1 yardstick	7 step ladder	14 fuses	21 paint
2 fly swatter	8 mousetrap	15 oil	22 paint thinner
3 plunger	9 masking tape	16 glue	23 paintbrush/brush
4 flashlight	10 electrical tape	17 work gloves	24 paint pan
5 extension cord	11 duct tape	18 bug spray/insect spray	25 paint roller
6 tape measure	12 batteries	19 roach killer	26 spray gun
	13 lightbulbs/bulbs	20 sandpaper	

A. I can't find the **yardstick**!
B. Look in the utility cabinet.
A. I did.
B. Oh! Wait a minute! I lent the **yardstick** to the neighbors.

[1–8, 23–26]
A. I'm going to the hardware store. Can you think of anything we need?
B. Yes. We need a/an _____.
A. Oh, that's right.

[9–22]
A. I'm going to the hardware store. Can you think of anything we need?
B. Yes. We need _____.
A. Oh, that's right.

What home supplies do you have? How and when do you use each one?

1 hammer	9 wrench	16 pliers	23 router
2 mallet	10 monkey wrench/	17 toolbox	24 wire
3 ax	pipe wrench	18 plane	25 nail
4 saw/handsaw	11 chisel	19 electric drill	26 washer
5 hacksaw	12 scraper	20 (drill) bit	27 nut
6 level	13 wire stripper	21 circular saw/	28 wood screw
7 screwdriver	14 hand drill	power saw	29 machine screw
8 Phillips screwdriver	15 vise	22 power sander	30 bolt

A. Can I borrow your **hammer**?
B. Sure.
A. Thanks.

With 25–30, use: Could I borrow some _____s?

[1–15, 17–24]
A. Where's the _____?
B. It's on/next to/near/over/under the _____.

[16, 25–30]
A. Where are the _____s?
B. They're on/next to/near/over/under the _____.

Do you like to work with tools? What tools do you have in your home?

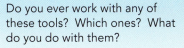

A mow the lawn	**1** lawnmower	**8** wheelbarrow	**15** leaf blower
B plant vegetables	**2** gas can	**9** fertilizer	**16** yard waste bag
C plant flowers	**3** line trimmer	**10** (garden) hose	**17** (hedge) clippers
D water the flowers	**4** shovel	**11** nozzle	**18** hedge trimmer
E rake leaves	**5** vegetable seeds	**12** sprinkler	**19** pruning shears
F trim the hedge	**6** hoe	**13** watering can	**20** weeder
G prune the bushes	**7** trowel	**14** rake	
H weed			

[A–H]
A. Hi! Are you busy?
B. Yes. I'm **mow**ing **the lawn**.

[1–20]
A. What are you looking for?
B. The **lawnmower**.

[A–H]
A. What are you going to do tomorrow?
B. I'm going to _____ .

[1–20]
A. Can I borrow your _____?
B. Sure.

Do you ever work with any of these tools? Which ones? What do you do with them?

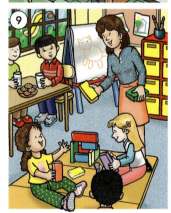

1 bakery
2 bank
3 barber shop
4 book store

5 bus station
6 candy store
7 car dealership
8 card store

9 child-care center / day-care center
10 cleaners / dry cleaners
11 clinic
12 clothing store

13 coffee shop
14 computer store
15 convenience store
16 copy center

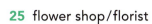

17 delicatessen/deli	**21** drug store/pharmacy	**25** flower shop/florist
18 department store	**22** electronics store	**26** furniture store
19 discount store	**23** eye-care center/optician	**27** gas station/service station
20 donut shop	**24** fast-food restaurant	**28** grocery store

A. Where are you going?
B. I'm going to the **bakery**.

A. Hi! How are you today?
B. Fine. Where are you going?
A. To the _____. How about you?
B. I'm going to the _____.

A. Oh, no! I can't find my wallet/purse!
B. Did you leave it at the _____?
A. Maybe I did.

Which of these places are in your neighborhood?
(In my neighborhood there's a/an ....)

1 hair salon	**5** hotel	**9** library	**13** music store
2 hardware store	**6** ice cream shop	**10** maternity shop	**14** nail salon
3 health club	**7** jewelry store	**11** motel	**15** park
4 hospital	**8** laundromat	**12** movie theater	**16** pet shop/pet store

17 photo shop
18 pizza shop
19 post office
20 restaurant

21 school
22 shoe store
23 (shopping) mall
24 supermarket

25 toy store
26 train station
27 travel agency
28 video store

A. Where's the **hair salon**?
B. It's right over there.

A. Is there a/an _____ nearby?
B. Yes. There's a/an _____ around the corner.
A. Thanks.

A. Excuse me. Where's the _____?
B. It's down the street, next to the _____.
A. Thank you.

Which of these places are in your neighborhood?
(In my neighborhood there's a/an ....)

1 courthouse
2 taxi / cab / taxicab
3 taxi stand
4 taxi driver / cab driver
5 fire hydrant
6 trash container

7 city hall
8 fire alarm box
9 mailbox
10 sewer
11 police station

12 jail
13 sidewalk
14 street
15 street light
16 parking lot

17 meter maid
18 parking meter
19 garbage truck
20 subway
21 subway station

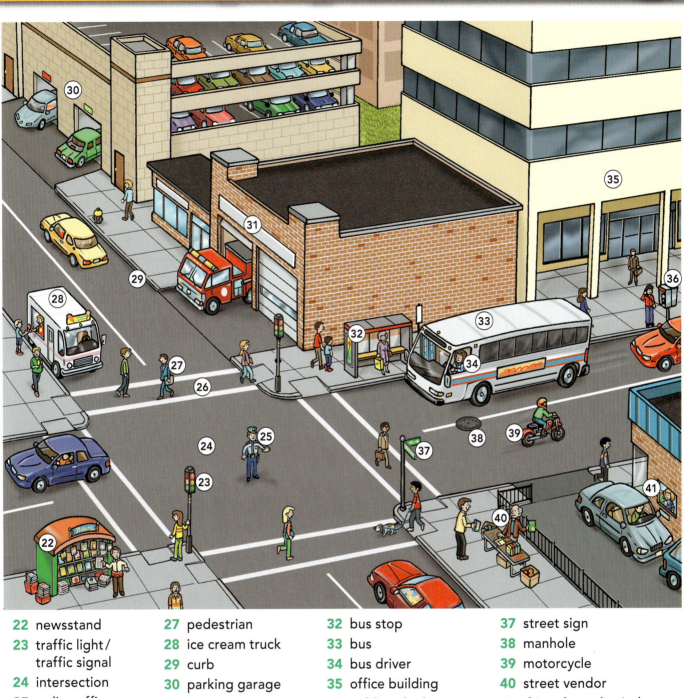

22 newsstand	**27** pedestrian	**32** bus stop	**37** street sign
23 traffic light / traffic signal	**28** ice cream truck	**33** bus	**38** manhole
24 intersection	**29** curb	**34** bus driver	**39** motorcycle
25 police officer	**30** parking garage	**35** office building	**40** street vendor
26 crosswalk	**31** fire station	**36** public telephone	**41** drive-through window

A. Where's the _____?
B. On / In / Next to / Between / Across from / In front of / Behind / Under / Over the _____.

[An Election Speech]

If I am elected mayor, I'll take care of all the problems in our city. We need to do something about our _____s. We also need to do something about our _____s. And look at our _____s! We REALLY need to do something about THEM! We need a new mayor who can solve these problems. If I am elected mayor, we'll be proud of our _____s, _____s, and _____s again! Vote for me!

Go to an intersection in your city or town. What do you see? Make a list. Then tell about it.

1 **child–children**
2 baby / infant
3 toddler
4 boy
5 girl
6 teenager

7 **adult**
8 man–men
9 woman–women
10 senior citizen / elderly person

age
11 young
12 middle-aged
13 old / elderly

height
14 tall
15 average height
16 short

weight
17 heavy
18 average weight
19 thin / slim

20 pregnant

21 physically challenged
22 vision impaired
23 hearing impaired

Describing Hair

24 long
25 shoulder length
26 short

27 straight
28 wavy
29 curly

30 black
31 brown
32 blond
33 red
34 gray

35 bald

36 beard
37 mustache

A. Tell me about *your brother*.
B. *He's a tall heavy boy* with *short curly brown* hair.

A. What does *your new boss* look like?
B. *She's average height*, and *she* has *long straight black* hair.

A. Can you describe *the person*?
B. *He's a tall thin middle-aged man*.
A. Anything else?
B. Yes. *He's bald*, and *he* has *a mustache*.

A. Can you describe *your grandmother*?
B. *She's a short thin elderly person* with *long wavy gray* hair.
A. Anything else?
B. Yes. *She's hearing impaired*.

Tell about yourself.

Tell about people in your family.

Tell about your favorite actor or actress or other famous person.

1–2 new – old		**25–26** dark – light	
3–4 young – old		**27–28** high – low	
5–6 tall – short		**29–30** loose – tight	
7–8 long – short		**31–32** good – bad	
9–10 large/big – small/little		**33–34** hot – cold	
11–12 fast – slow		**35–36** neat – messy	
13–14 heavy/fat – thin/skinny		**37–38** clean – dirty	
15–16 heavy – light		**39–40** soft – hard	
17–18 straight – crooked		**41–42** easy – difficult/hard	
19–20 straight – curly		**43–44** smooth – rough	
21–22 wide – narrow		**45–46** noisy/loud – quiet	
23–24 thick – thin		**47–48** married – single	

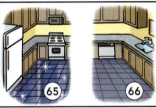  

49–50	rich/wealthy – poor	**61–62**	expensive – cheap/inexpensive
51–52	pretty/beautiful – ugly	**63–64**	fancy – plain
53–54	handsome – ugly	**65–66**	shiny – dull
55–56	wet – dry	**67–68**	sharp – dull
57–58	open – closed	**69–70**	comfortable – uncomfortable
59–60	full – empty	**71–72**	honest – dishonest

[1–2]
A. Is your car **new**?
B. No. It's **old**.

1–2	Is your car _____?
3–4	Is he _____?
5–6	Is your sister _____?
7–8	Is his hair _____?
9–10	Is their dog _____?
11–12	Is the train _____?
13–14	Is your friend _____?
15–16	Is the box _____?
17–18	Is the road _____?
19–20	Is her hair _____?
21–22	Is the tie _____?
23–24	Is the line _____?
25–26	Is the room _____?
27–28	Is the bridge _____?
29–30	Are the pants _____?
31–32	Are your neighbor's children _____?
33–34	Is the water _____?
35–36	Is your desk _____?

37–38	Are the windows _____?
39–40	Is the mattress _____?
41–42	Is the homework _____?
43–44	Is your skin _____?
45–46	Is your neighbor _____?
47–48	Is your sister _____?
49–50	Is your uncle _____?
51–52	Is the witch _____?
53–54	Is the pirate _____?
55–56	Are the clothes _____?
57–58	Is the door _____?
59–60	Is the pitcher _____?
61–62	Is that restaurant _____?
63–64	Is the dress _____?
65–66	Is your kitchen floor _____?
67–68	Is the knife _____?
69–70	Is the chair _____?
71–72	Is he _____?

A. Tell me about your ………
B. He's/She's/It's/They're _____.

A. Do you have a/an _____ ………?
B. No. I have a/an _____ ……….

Describe yourself.
Describe a person you know.
Describe some things in your home.
Describe some things in your community.

1 tired	5 hot	9 full	13 excited
2 sleepy	6 cold	10 happy	14 disappointed
3 exhausted	7 hungry	11 sad / unhappy	15 upset
4 sick / ill	8 thirsty	12 miserable	16 annoyed

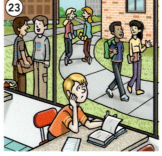

17 angry / mad	**21** surprised	**25** nervous	**29** proud
18 furious	**22** shocked	**26** worried	**30** embarrassed
19 disgusted	**23** lonely	**27** scared / afraid	**31** jealous
20 frustrated	**24** homesick	**28** bored	**32** confused

A. You look _____.
B. I am. I'm VERY _____.

A. Are you _____?
B. No. Why do you ask? Do I LOOK _____?
A. Yes. You do.

What makes you happy? sad? mad?

What do you do when you feel nervous? annoyed?

Do you ever feel embarrassed? When?

1 apple	7 apricot	14 avocado	20 lemon	27 dates
2 peach	8 nectarine	15 cantaloupe	21 lime	28 raisins
3 pear	9 kiwi	16 honeydew (melon)	22 orange	29 nuts
4 banana	10 papaya	17 watermelon	23 tangerine	30 raspberries
5 plantain	11 mango	18 pineapple	24 grapes	31 blueberries
6 plum	12 fig	19 grapefruit	25 cherries	32 strawberries
	13 coconut		26 prunes	

[1–23]

A. This **apple** is delicious! Where did you get it?

B. At *Sam's Supermarket.*

[24–32]

A. These **grapes** are delicious! Where did you get them?

B. At *Franny's Fruit Stand.*

A. I'm hungry. Do we have any fruit?

B. Yes. We have _____s* and _____s.*

* With 15–19, use:
We have _____ and _____ .

A. Do we have any more _____s?†

B. No. I'll get some more when I go to the supermarket.

† With 15–19 use:
Do we have any more _____?

What are your favorite fruits?
Which fruits don't you like?

Which of these fruits grow where you live?

Name and describe other fruits you know.

1 celery	**11** bok choy	**21** brussels sprout	**31** green pepper/
2 corn	**12** zucchini	**22** cucumber	sweet pepper
3 broccoli	**13** acorn squash	**23** tomato	**32** red pepper
4 cauliflower	**14** butternut squash	**24** carrot	**33** jalapeño (pepper)
5 spinach	**15** garlic	**25** radish	**34** chili pepper
6 parsley	**16** pea	**26** mushroom	**35** beet
7 asparagus	**17** string bean/green bean	**27** artichoke	**36** onion
8 eggplant	**18** lima bean	**28** potato	**37** scallion/green onion
9 lettuce	**19** black bean	**29** sweet potato	**38** turnip
10 cabbage	**20** kidney bean	**30** yam	

A. What do we need from the supermarket?
B. We need **celery*** and **pea**s.†

* 1–15   † 16–38

A. How do you like the
   __[1–15]__ / __[16–38]__s?
B. It's/They're delicious.

A. *Bobby*? Finish your vegetables!
B. But you KNOW I hate
   __[1–15]__ / __[16–38]__s!
A. I know. But it's/they're good for you!

Which vegetables do you like?
Which vegetables don't you like?

Which of these vegetables grow where you live?

Name and describe other vegetables you know.

Meat

1 steak
2 ground beef
3 stewing beef
4 roast beef
5 ribs
6 leg of lamb
7 lamb chops
8 tripe
9 liver
10 pork
11 pork chops
12 sausages
13 ham
14 bacon

Poultry

15 chicken
16 chicken breasts
17 chicken legs/ drumsticks
18 chicken wings
19 chicken thighs
20 turkey
21 duck

Seafood

FISH

22 salmon
23 halibut
24 haddock
25 flounder
26 trout
27 catfish
28 filet of sole

SHELLFISH

29 shrimp
30 scallops
31 crabs
32 clams
33 mussels
34 oysters
35 lobster

A. I'm going to the supermarket. What do we need?
B. Please get some **steak**.
A. **Steak**? All right.

A. Excuse me. Where can I find _____?
B. Look in the _____ Section.
A. Thank you.

A. This/These _____ looks/ look very fresh!
B. Let's get some for dinner.

Do you eat meat, poultry, or seafood? Which of these foods do you like?

Which of these foods are popular in your country?

Dairy Products

1 milk
2 low-fat milk
3 skim milk
4 chocolate milk
5 orange juice*
6 cheese
7 butter
8 margarine
9 sour cream
10 cream cheese
11 cottage cheese
12 yogurt
13 tofu*
14 eggs

*Orange juice and tofu are not dairy products, but they're usually found in this section.

Juices

15 apple juice
16 pineapple juice
17 grapefruit juice
18 tomato juice
19 grape juice
20 fruit punch
21 juice paks
22 powdered drink mix

Beverages

23 soda
24 diet soda
25 bottled water

Coffee and Tea

26 coffee
27 decaffeinated coffee/decaf
28 instant coffee
29 tea
30 herbal tea
31 cocoa/ hot chocolate mix

A. I'm going to the supermarket to get some **milk**. Do we need anything else?
B. Yes. Please get some **apple juice**.

A. Excuse me. Where can I find _____?
B. Look in the _____ Section.
A. Thanks.

A. Look! _____ is/are on sale this week!
B. Let's get some!

Which of these foods do you like?

Which of these foods are good for you?

Which brands of these foods do you buy?

Deli

1 roast beef	7 pastrami	13 potato salad
2 bologna	8 Swiss cheese	14 cole slaw
3 salami	9 provolone	15 macaroni salad
4 ham	10 American cheese	16 pasta salad
5 turkey	11 mozzarella	17 seafood salad
6 corned beef	12 cheddar cheese	

Frozen Foods

18 ice cream
19 frozen vegetables
20 frozen dinners
21 frozen lemonade
22 frozen orange juice

Snack Foods

23 potato chips
24 tortilla chips
25 pretzels
26 nuts
27 popcorn

A. Should we get some **roast beef**?
B. Good idea. And let's get some **potato salad**.

[1–17]
A. May I help you?
B. Yes, please. I'd like some _____.

[1–27]
A. Excuse me. Where is/are _____?
B. It's/They're in the _____ Section.

What kinds of snack foods are popular in your country?

Are frozen foods common in your country? What kinds of foods are in the Frozen Foods Section?

Packaged Goods
1 cereal
2 cookies
3 crackers
4 macaroni
5 noodles
6 spaghetti
7 rice

Canned Goods
8 soup
9 tuna (fish)
10 (canned) vegetables
11 (canned) fruit

Jams and Jellies
12 jam
13 jelly
14 peanut butter

Condiments
15 ketchup
16 mustard
17 relish
18 pickles
19 olives
20 salt
21 pepper
22 spices

23 soy sauce
24 mayonnaise
25 (cooking) oil
26 olive oil
27 salsa
28 vinegar
29 salad dressing

Baked Goods
30 bread
31 rolls
32 English muffins
33 pita bread
34 cake

Baking Products
35 flour
36 sugar
37 cake mix

A. I got **cereal** and **soup**. What else is on the shopping list?
B. **Ketchup** and **bread**.

A. Excuse me. I'm looking for _____.
B. It's/They're next to the _____.

A. Pardon me. I'm looking for _____.
B. It's/They're between the _____ and the _____.

Which of these foods do you like?

Which brands of these foods do you buy?

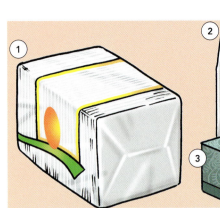
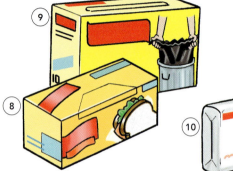
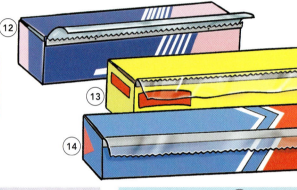

Paper Products	Household Items	Baby Products	Pet Food
1 napkins	8 sandwich bags	15 baby cereal	20 cat food
2 paper cups	9 trash bags	16 baby food	21 dog food
3 tissues	10 soap	17 formula	
4 straws	11 liquid soap	18 wipes	
5 paper plates	12 aluminum foil	19 (disposable) diapers	
6 paper towels	13 plastic wrap		
7 toilet paper	14 waxed paper		

A. Excuse me. Where can I find **napkins**?
B. **Napkins**? Look in Aisle 4.

[7, 10–17, 20, 21]
A. We forgot to get _____!
B. I'll get it. Where is it?
A. It's in Aisle _____.

[1–6, 8, 9, 18, 19]
A. We forgot to get _____!
B. I'll get them. Where are they?
A. They're in Aisle _____.

What do you need from the supermarket? Make a complete shopping list!

1 aisle	**8** shopping cart	**15** express checkout (line)	**22** clerk
2 shopper/customer	**9** (chewing) gum	**16** tabloid (newspaper)	**23** scale
3 shopping basket	**10** candy	**17** magazine	**24** can-return machine
4 checkout line	**11** coupons	**18** scanner	**25** bottle-return machine
5 checkout counter	**12** cashier	**19** plastic bag	
6 conveyor belt	**13** paper bag	**20** produce	
7 cash register	**14** bagger/packer	**21** manager	

[1–8, 11–19, 21–25]
A. This is a gigantic supermarket!
B. It is! Look at all the **aisle**s!

[9, 10, 20]
A. This is a gigantic supermarket!
B. It is. Look at all the **produce**!

Where do you usually shop for food? Do you go to a supermarket, or do you go to a small grocery store? Describe the place where you shop.

Describe the differences between U.S. supermarkets and food stores in your country.

1 bag	**5** can	**9** head	**14** roll	**18** pint
2 bottle	**6** carton	**10** jar	**15** six-pack	**19** quart
3 box	**7** container	**11** loaf–loaves	**16** stick	**20** half-gallon
4 bunch	**8** dozen*	**12** pack	**17** tube	**21** gallon
		13 package		**22** liter
				23 pound

* "a dozen eggs," NOT "a dozen of eggs"

A. Please get a **bag** of *flour* when you go to the supermarket.
B. A **bag** of *flour*? Okay.

A. Please get two **bottles** of *ketchup* when you go to the supermarket.
B. Two **bottles** of *ketchup*? Okay.

[At home]
A. What did you get at the supermarket?
B. I got _____, _____, and _____.

[In a supermarket]
A. Is this the express checkout line?
B. Yes, it is. Do you have more than eight items?
A. No. I only have _____, _____, and _____.

Open your kitchen cabinets and refrigerator. Make a list of all the things you find.

What do you do with empty bottles, jars, and cans? Do you recycle them, reuse them, or throw them away?

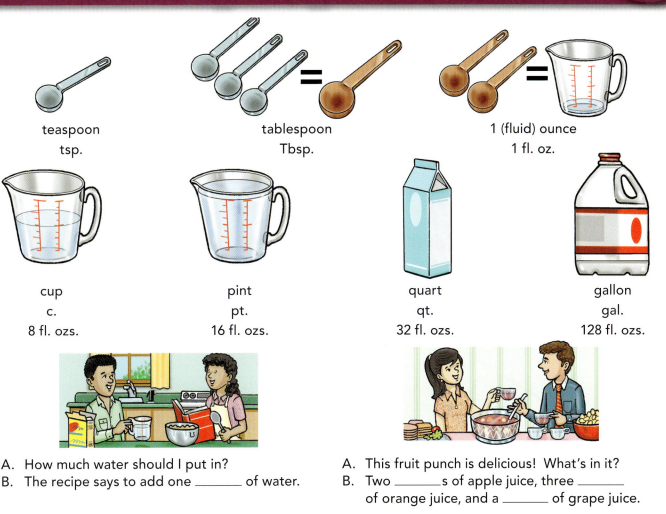

teaspoon
tsp.

tablespoon
Tbsp.

1 (fluid) ounce
1 fl. oz.

cup
c.
8 fl. ozs.

pint
pt.
16 fl. ozs.

quart
qt.
32 fl. ozs.

gallon
gal.
128 fl. ozs.

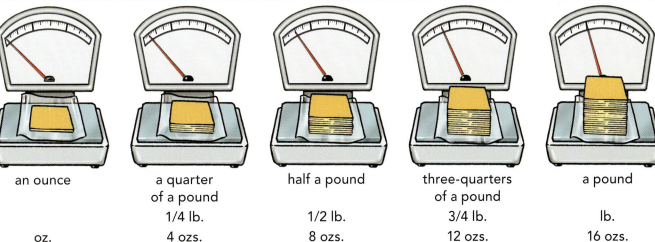

A. How much water should I put in?
B. The recipe says to add one _____ of water.

A. This fruit punch is delicious! What's in it?
B. Two _____s of apple juice, three _____ of orange juice, and a _____ of grape juice.

an ounce

oz.

a quarter
of a pound
1/4 lb.
4 ozs.

half a pound

1/2 lb.
8 ozs.

three-quarters
of a pound
3/4 lb.
12 ozs.

a pound

lb.
16 ozs.

A. How much roast beef would you like?
B. I'd like _____, please.
A. Anything else?
B. Yes. Please give me _____ of Swiss cheese.

A. This chili tastes very good! What did you put in it?
B. _____ of ground beef, _____ of beans, _____ of tomatoes, and _____ of chili powder.

1	cut (up)	6	break	11	combine _____ and _____	16	boil	21	simmer
2	chop (up)	7	beat	12	mix _____ and _____	17	broil	22	roast
3	slice	8	stir	13	put _____ in _____	18	steam	23	barbecue / grill
4	grate	9	pour	14	cook	19	fry	24	stir-fry
5	peel	10	add	15	bake	20	saute	25	microwave

A. Can I help you?
B. Yes. Please **cut up** the vegetables.

[1–25]
A. What are you doing?
B. I'm _____ing the …………..

[14–25]
A. How long should I _____ the …………?
B. _____ the …………. for …………. minutes / seconds.

What's your favorite recipe? Give instructions and use the units of measure on page 57. For example:

  Mix a cup of flour and two tablespoons of sugar.
  Add half a pound of butter.
  Bake at 350° (degrees) for twenty minutes.

1 ice cream scoop	**10** wok	**19** roasting pan	**28** cookie sheet
2 can opener	**11** ladle	**20** roasting rack	**29** cookie cutter
3 bottle opener	**12** strainer	**21** carving knife	**30** (mixing) bowl
4 (vegetable) peeler	**13** spatula	**22** saucepan	**31** whisk
5 (egg) beater	**14** steamer	**23** colander	**32** measuring cup
6 lid/cover/top	**15** knife	**24** kitchen timer	**33** measuring spoon
7 pot	**16** garlic press	**25** rolling pin	**34** cake pan
8 frying pan/skillet	**17** grater	**26** pie plate	**35** wooden spoon
9 double boiler	**18** casserole dish	**27** paring knife	

A. Could I possibly borrow your **ice cream scoop**?
B. Sure. I'll be happy to lend you my **ice cream scoop**.
A. Thanks.

A. What are you looking for?
B. I can't find the _____.
A. Look in that drawer/in that cabinet/ on the counter/next to the _____/
....

[A Commercial]
Come to *Kitchen World*! We have everything you need for your kitchen, from _____s and _____s, to _____s and _____s. Are you looking for a new _____? Is it time to throw out your old _____? Come to *Kitchen World* today! We have everything you need!

What kitchen utensils and cookware do you have in your kitchen?

Which things do you use very often?

Which things do you rarely use?

1 hamburger
2 cheeseburger
3 hot dog
4 fish sandwich
5 chicken sandwich
6 fried chicken
7 french fries

8 nachos
9 taco
10 burrito
11 slice of pizza
12 bowl of chili
13 salad
14 ice cream

15 frozen yogurt
16 milkshake
17 soda
18 lids
19 paper cups
20 straws
21 napkins

22 plastic utensils
23 ketchup
24 mustard
25 mayonnaise
26 relish
27 salad dressing

A. May I help you?
B. Yes. I'd like a/an ___[1–5, 9–17]___ /
an order of ___[6–8]___ .

A. Excuse me. We're almost out
of ___[18–27]___ .
B. I'll get some more from the
supply room. Thanks for
telling me.

Do you go to fast-food restaurants? Which ones? How often? What do you order?

Are there fast-food restaurants in your country? Are they popular? What foods do they have?

1 donut	8 eggs	15 coffee	22 tuna fish sandwich	29 white bread
2 muffin	9 pancakes	16 decaf coffee	23 egg salad sandwich	30 whole wheat bread
3 bagel	10 waffles	17 tea	24 chicken salad sandwich	31 pita bread
4 bun	11 toast	18 iced tea	25 ham and cheese sandwich	32 pumpernickel
5 danish/pastry	12 bacon	19 lemonade	26 corned beef sandwich	33 rye bread
6 biscuit	13 sausages	20 hot chocolate	27 BLT/bacon, lettuce, and tomato sandwich	34 a roll
7 croissant	14 home fries	21 milk	28 roast beef sandwich	35 a submarine roll

A. May I help you?
B. Yes. I'd like a ___[1–7]___/ an order of ___[8–14]___, please.
A. Anything to drink?
B. Yes. I'll have a small/medium-size/ large/extra-large ___[15–21]___.

A. I'd like a ___[22–28]___ on ___[29–35]___, please.
B. What do you want on it?
A. Lettuce/tomato/mayonnaise/mustard/. . .

Do you like these foods? Which ones? Where do you get them? How often do you have them?

A seat the customers	**1** hostess	**7** booster seat	**13** salad bar
B pour the water	**2** host	**8** menu	**14** dining room
C take the order	**3** diner / patron / customer	**9** bread basket	**15** kitchen
D serve the meal	**4** booth	**10** busperson	**16** chef
	5 table	**11** waitress / server	
	6 high chair	**12** waiter / server	

[4–9]
A. Would you like a **booth**?
B. Yes, please.

[10–12]
A. Hello. My name is *Julie*, and I'll be your **waitress** this evening.
B. Hello.

[1, 2, 13–16]
A. This restaurant has a wonderful **salad bar**.
B. I agree.

E clear the table	**17** dishroom	**23** salad plate	**31** napkin
F pay the check	**18** dishwasher	**24** bread-and-butter plate	**silverware**
G leave a tip	**19** tray	**25** dinner plate	**32** salad fork
H set the table	**20** dessert cart	**26** soup bowl	**33** dinner fork
	21 check	**27** water glass	**34** knife
	22 tip	**28** wine glass	**35** teaspoon
		29 cup	**36** soup spoon
		30 saucer	**37** butter knife

[A–H]
A. Please _____.
B. All right. I'll _____ right away.

[23–37]
A. Excuse me. Where does the _____ go?
B. It goes
{
to the left of the _____.
to the right of the _____.
on the _____.
between the _____ and the _____.
}

[1, 2, 10–12, 16, 18]
A. Do you have any job openings?
B. Yes. We're looking for a
_____.

[23–37]
A. Excuse me. I dropped my _____.
B. That's okay. I'll get you another
_____ from the kitchen.

Tell about a restaurant you know.
Describe the place and the people. (Is
the restaurant large or small? How many
tables are there? How many people work
there? Is there a salad bar? . . .)

ENTREES

APPETIZERS

SALADS

SIDE DISHES

DESSERTS

1. fruit cup/
   fruit cocktail
2. tomato juice
3. shrimp cocktail
4. chicken wings
5. nachos
6. potato skins

7. tossed salad/
   garden salad
8. Greek salad
9. spinach salad
10. antipasto (plate)
11. Caesar salad

12. meatloaf
13. roast beef/
    prime rib
14. baked chicken
15. broiled fish
16. spaghetti and
    meatballs
17. veal cutlet

18. a baked
    potato
19. mashed
    potatoes
20. french fries
21. rice
22. noodles
23. mixed
    vegetables

24. chocolate cake
25. apple pie
26. ice cream
27. jello
28. pudding
29. ice cream
    sundae

[Ordering dinner]

A. May I take your order?
B. Yes, please. For the appetizer, I'd like the ____[1–6]____.
A. And what kind of salad would you like?
B. I'll have the ____[7–11]____.
A. And for the main course?
B. I'd like the ____[12–17]____, please.
A. What side dish would you like with that?
B. Hmm. I think I'll have ____[18–23]____.

[Ordering dessert]

A. Would you care for some dessert?
B. Yes. I'll have ____[24–28]____/an ____[29]____.

Tell about the food at a restaurant you know. What's on the menu?

What are some typical foods on the menus of restaurants in your country?

1. red
2. pink
3. orange
4. yellow
5. brown
6. beige
7. blue
8. navy blue
9. turquoise
10. green
11. light green
12. dark green
13. purple
14. black
15. white
16. gray
17. silver
18. gold

A. What's your favorite color?
B. **Red**.

A. I like your _____ shirt.
You look very good in _____.
B. Thank you. _____ is my favorite color.

A. My TV is broken.
B. What's the matter with it?
A. People's faces are _____, the sky is _____, and the grass is _____!

Do you know the flags of different countries? What are the colors of flags you know?

What color makes you happy? What color makes you sad? Why?

1 blouse	**9** sweater	**15** uniform	**23** tunic
2 skirt	**10** jacket	**16** T-shirt	**24** leggings
3 shirt	**11** sport coat / sport jacket /	**17** shorts	**25** overalls
4 pants / slacks	jacket	**18** maternity dress	**26** turtleneck
5 sport shirt	**12** suit	**19** jumpsuit	**27** tuxedo
6 jeans	**13** three-piece suit	**20** vest	**28** bow tie
7 knit shirt / jersey	**14** tie / necktie	**21** jumper	**29** (evening) gown
8 dress		**22** blazer	

A. I think I'll wear my new **blouse** today.
B. Good idea!

A. I really like your _____.
B. Thank you.
A. Where did you get it / them?
B. At ....

A. Oh, no! I just ripped
my _____!
B. What a shame!

What clothing items in this lesson do you wear?

What color clothing do you like to wear?

What do you wear at work or at school? at parties? at weddings?

1 coat	8 cap	15 umbrella	22 ski mask
2 overcoat	9 leather jacket	16 poncho	23 down jacket
3 hat	10 baseball cap	17 rain jacket	24 mittens
4 jacket	11 windbreaker	18 rain boots	25 parka
5 scarf/muffler	12 raincoat	19 ski hat	26 sunglasses
6 sweater jacket	13 rain hat	20 ski jacket	27 ear muffs
7 tights	14 trench coat	21 gloves	28 down vest

A. What's the weather like today?
B. It's cool/cold/raining/snowing.
A. I think I'll wear my _____ .

[1–6, 8–17, 19, 20, 22, 23, 25, 28]
A. May I help you?
B. Yes, please. I'm looking for a/an _____ .

[7, 18, 21, 24, 26, 27]
A. May I help you?
B. Yes, please. I'm looking for _____ .

What do you wear outside when the weather is cool?/when it's raining?/when it's very cold?

1 pajamas	7 undershirt/T-shirt	13 (bikini) panties	19 stockings
2 nightgown	8 (jockey) shorts/underpants/	14 briefs/underpants	20 pantyhose
3 nightshirt	briefs	15 bra	21 tights
4 bathrobe/robe	9 boxer shorts/boxers	16 camisole	22 knee-highs
5 slippers	10 athletic supporter/jockstrap	17 half slip	23 knee socks
6 blanket sleeper	11 long underwear/long johns	18 (full) slip	
	12 socks		

A. I can't find my new _____.
B. Did you look in the bureau/dresser/closet?
A. Yes, I did.
B. Then it's/they're probably in the wash.

What sleepwear items do you wear? What sleepwear items do people in your family wear?

1 tank top
2 running shorts
3 sweatband
4 jogging suit/
running suit/
warm-up suit
5 T-shirt
6 lycra shorts/
bike shorts

7 sweatshirt
8 sweatpants
9 cover-up
10 swimsuit/bathing suit
11 swimming trunks/
swimsuit/
bathing suit
12 leotard

13 shoes
14 (high) heels
15 pumps
16 loafers
17 sneakers/athletic shoes
18 tennis shoes
19 running shoes
20 high-tops/high-top
sneakers

21 sandals
22 thongs/
flip-flops
23 boots
24 work boots
25 hiking boots
26 cowboy boots
27 moccasins

[1–12]
A. Excuse me. I found this/these _____
in the dryer. Is it/Are they yours?
B. Yes. It's/They're mine. Thank you.

[13–27]
A. Are those new _____?
B. Yes, they are.
A. They're very nice.
B. Thanks.

Do you exercise? What do you do? What kind of clothing do you wear when you exercise?

What kind of shoes do you wear when you go to work or to school? when you exercise?
when you relax at home? when you go out with friends or family members?

1 ring	**7** chain	**14** suspenders	**21** purse/handbag/ pocketbook
2 engagement ring	**8** beads	**15** watch/wrist watch	**22** shoulder bag
3 wedding ring/wedding band	**9** pin/brooch	**16** handkerchief	**23** tote bag
4 earrings	**10** locket	**17** key ring/key chain	**24** book bag
5 necklace	**11** bracelet	**18** change purse	**25** backpack
6 pearl necklace/pearls/ string of pearls	**12** barrette	**19** wallet	**26** makeup bag
	13 cuff links	**20** belt	**27** briefcase

A. Oh, no! I think I lost my **ring**!
B. I'll help you look for it.

A. Oh, no! I think I lost my **earrings**!
B. I'll help you look for them.

[In a store]
A. Excuse me. Is this/Are these _____ on sale this week?
B. Yes. It's/They're half price.

[On the street]
A. Help! Police! Stop that man/woman!
B. What happened?!
A. He/She just stole my _____ and my _____!

Do you like to wear jewelry? What jewelry do you have?

In your country, what do men, women, and children use to carry their things?

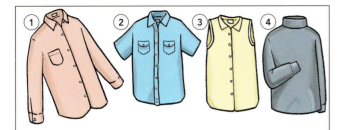

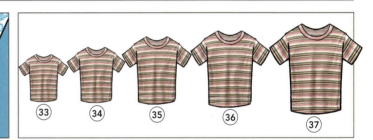

Types of Clothing
1 long-sleeved shirt
2 short-sleeved shirt
3 sleeveless shirt
4 turtleneck (shirt)

5 V-neck sweater
6 cardigan sweater
7 crewneck sweater
8 turtleneck sweater

9 knee-high socks
10 ankle socks
11 crew socks

12 pierced earrings
13 clip-on earrings

Types of Material
14 corduroy *pants*
15 leather *boots*
16 nylon *stockings*

17 cotton *T-shirt*
18 denim *jacket*
19 flannel *shirt*
20 polyester *blouse*
21 linen *dress*
22 silk *scarf*
23 wool *sweater*
24 straw *hat*

Patterns
25 striped
26 checked
27 plaid
28 polka-dotted
29 patterned/ print
30 flowered/ floral
31 paisley
32 solid *blue*

Sizes
33 extra-small
34 small
35 medium
36 large
37 extra-large

[1–24]
A. May I help you?
B. Yes, please. I'm looking for a *shirt*.*
A. What kind?
B. I'm looking for a *long-sleeved shirt*.

* With 9–16: I'm looking for _____.

[25–32]
A. How do you like this _____ tie/shirt/skirt?
B. Actually, I prefer that _____ one.

[33–37]
A. What size are you looking for?
B. _____.

Describe your favorite clothing items. For each item, tell about the color, the type of material, the size, and the pattern.

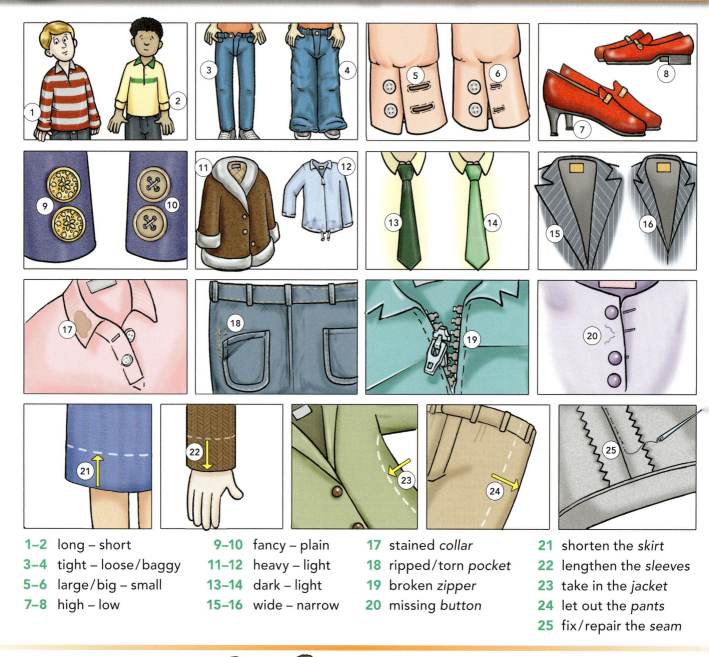

1–2 long – short	**9–10** fancy – plain	**17** stained *collar*	**21** shorten the *skirt*
3–4 tight – loose/baggy	**11–12** heavy – light	**18** ripped/torn *pocket*	**22** lengthen the *sleeves*
5–6 large/big – small	**13–14** dark – light	**19** broken *zipper*	**23** take in the *jacket*
7–8 high – low	**15–16** wide – narrow	**20** missing *button*	**24** let out the *pants*
			25 fix/repair the *seam*

[1–2]
A. Are the sleeves too **long**?
B. No. They're too **short**.

1–2 Are the sleeves too _____?	9–10 Are the buttons too _____?
3–4 Are the pants too _____?	11–12 Is the coat too _____?
5–6 Are the buttonholes too _____?	13–14 Is the color too _____?
7–8 Are the heels too _____?	15–16 Are the lapels too _____?

[17–20]
A. What's the matter with it?
B. It has a **stained** collar.

[21–25]
A. Please **shorten** the *skirt*.
B. **Shorten** the *skirt*? Okay.

Tell about the differences between clothing people wear now and clothing people wore a long time ago.

A sort the laundry
B load the washer
C unload the washer
D load the dryer
E hang clothes on the clothesline
F iron
G fold the laundry
H hang up clothing
I put things away

1 laundry
2 light clothing
3 dark clothing
4 laundry basket
5 laundry bag
6 washer/washing machine
7 laundry detergent
8 fabric softener
9 bleach
10 wet clothing

11 dryer
12 lint trap
13 static cling remover
14 clothesline
15 clothespin
16 iron
17 ironing board
18 wrinkled clothing
19 ironed clothing

20 spray starch
21 clean clothing
22 closet
23 hanger
24 drawer
25 shelf-shelves

[A–I]
A. What are you doing?
B. I'm _____ing.

[4–6, 11, 14–17, 23]
A. Excuse me. Do you sell _____s?
B. Yes. They're at the back of the store.
A. Thank you.

[7–9, 13, 20]
A. Excuse me. Do you sell _____?
B. Yes. It's at the back of the store.
A. Thank you.

Who does the laundry in your home?
What things does this person use?

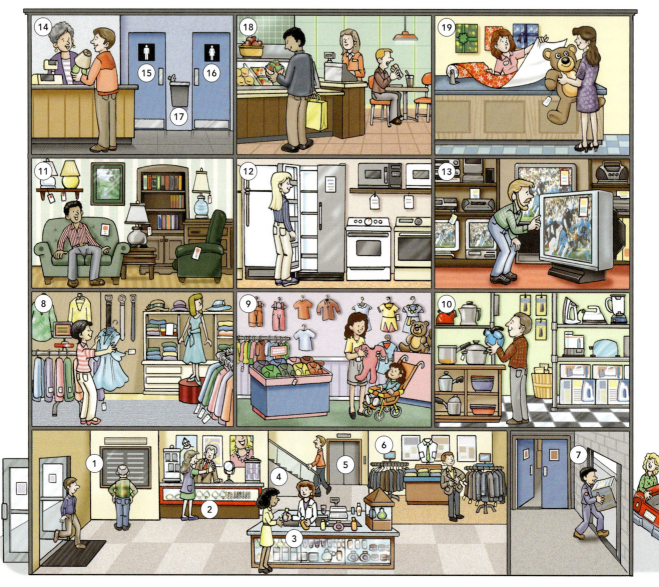

1 (store) directory
2 Jewelry Counter
3 Perfume Counter
4 escalator
5 elevator
6 Men's Clothing Department
7 customer pickup area

8 Women's Clothing Department
9 Children's Clothing Department
10 Housewares Department
11 Furniture Department/ Home Furnishings Department
12 Household Appliances Department
13 Electronics Department

14 Customer Assistance Counter/ Customer Service Counter
15 men's room
16 ladies' room
17 water fountain
18 snack bar
19 Gift Wrap Counter

A. Excuse me. Where's the **store directory**?
B. It's over there, next to the **Jewelry Counter**.
A. Thanks.
B. You're welcome.

A. Excuse me. Do you sell *ties*?
B. Yes. You can find *ties* in the ___[6, 8–13]___ /at the ___[2, 3]___ on the first/second/third/fourth floor.
A. Thank you.

*ties/bracelets/dresses/toasters/...

Describe a department store you know. Tell what is on each floor.

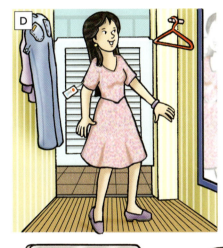

A buy
B return
C exchange
D try on
E pay for
F get some information about

1 sale sign
2 label
3 price tag
4 receipt

5 discount
6 size
7 material
8 care instructions

9 regular price
10 sale price
11 price
12 sales tax
13 total price

A. May I help you?
B. Yes, please. I want to _____[A–F]_____ this item.
A. Certainly. I'll be glad to help you.

A. { What's the _____[5–7, 9–13]_____?
    { What are the _____[8]_____?
B. _____.
A. Are you sure?
B. Yes. Look at the _____[1–4]_____!

Which stores in your area have sales? How often?

Tell about something you bought on sale.

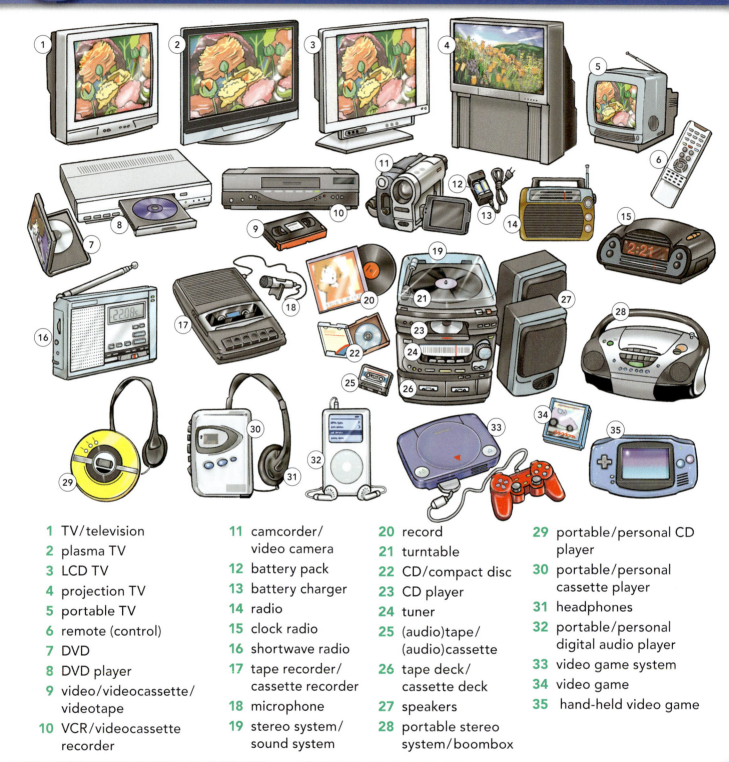

1 TV/television	11 camcorder/	20 record	29 portable/personal CD
2 plasma TV	video camera	21 turntable	player
3 LCD TV	12 battery pack	22 CD/compact disc	30 portable/personal
4 projection TV	13 battery charger	23 CD player	cassette player
5 portable TV	14 radio	24 tuner	31 headphones
6 remote (control)	15 clock radio	25 (audio)tape/	32 portable/personal
7 DVD	16 shortwave radio	(audio)cassette	digital audio player
8 DVD player	17 tape recorder/	26 tape deck/	33 video game system
9 video/videocassette/	cassette recorder	cassette deck	34 video game
videotape	18 microphone	27 speakers	35 hand-held video game
10 VCR/videocassette	19 stereo system/	28 portable stereo	
recorder	sound system	system/boombox	

A. May I help you?
B. Yes, please. I'm looking for a **TV**.

With 27 & 31, use: I'm looking for _____.

A. I like your new _____.
   Where did you get it/them?
B. At ....._(name of store)_....

A. Which company makes the best
   _____?
B. In my opinion, the best _____
   is/are made by ....

What video and audio equipment do you have or want?

In your opinion, which brands of video and audio equipment are the best?

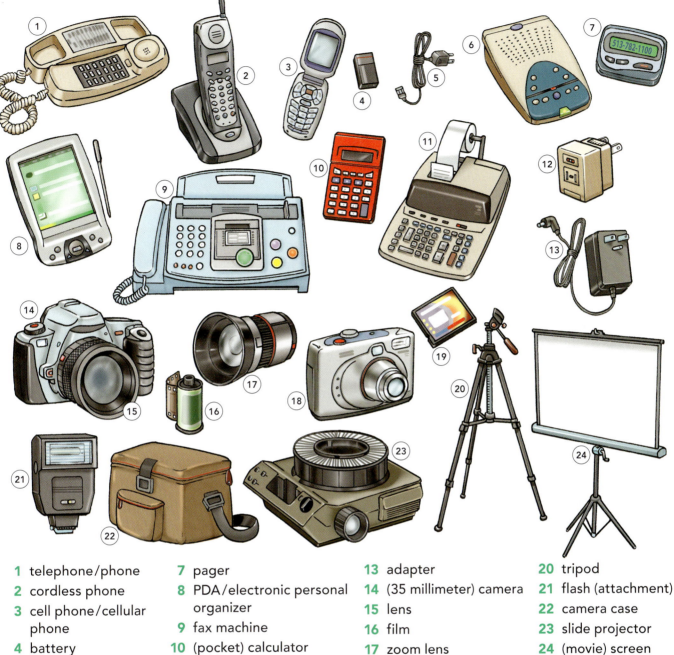

1 telephone/phone
2 cordless phone
3 cell phone/cellular phone
4 battery
5 battery charger
6 answering machine

7 pager
8 PDA/electronic personal organizer
9 fax machine
10 (pocket) calculator
11 adding machine
12 voltage regulator

13 adapter
14 (35 millimeter) camera
15 lens
16 film
17 zoom lens
18 digital camera
19 memory disk

20 tripod
21 flash (attachment)
22 camera case
23 slide projector
24 (movie) screen

A. Can I help you?
B. Yes. I want to buy a **telephone**.*

* With 16, use: I want to buy _____.

A. Excuse me. Do you sell _____s?*
B. Yes. We have a large selection of _____s.

* With 16, use the singular.

A. Which _____ is the best?
B. This one here. It's made by ......(company)......

What kind of telephone do you use?

Do you have a camera? What kind is it? What do you take pictures of?

Does anyone you know have an answering machine? When you call, what message do you hear?

Computer Hardware

1 (desktop) computer
2 CPU/central processing unit
3 monitor/screen
4 CD-ROM drive
5 CD-ROM
6 disk drive
7 (floppy) disk
8 keyboard
9 mouse
10 flat panel screen/ LCD screen
11 notebook computer
12 joystick
13 track ball
14 modem
15 surge protector
16 printer
17 scanner
18 cable

Computer Software

19 word-processing program
20 spreadsheet program
21 educational software program
22 computer game

A. Can you recommend a good **computer**?
B. Yes. This **computer** here is excellent.

A. Is that a new _____?
B. Yes.
A. Where did you get it?
B. At ....*(name of store)*..............

A. May I help you?
B. Yes, please. Do you sell _____s?
A. Yes. We carry a complete line of _____s.

Do you use a computer? When?

In your opinion, how have computers changed the world?

1 board game
2 (jigsaw) puzzle
3 construction set
4 (building) blocks
5 rubber ball
6 beach ball
7 pail and shovel
8 doll
9 doll clothing
10 doll house

11 doll house furniture
12 action figure
13 stuffed animal
14 matchbox car
15 toy truck
16 racing car set
17 train set
18 model kit
19 science kit
20 walkie-talkie (set)

21 hula hoop
22 jump rope
23 bubble soap
24 trading cards
25 crayons
26 (color) markers
27 coloring book
28 construction paper
29 paint set
30 (modeling) clay

31 stickers
32 bicycle
33 tricycle
34 wagon
35 skateboard
36 swing set
37 play house
38 kiddie pool/
   inflatable pool

A. Excuse me. I'm looking for (a/an) _____(s) for my *grandson*.*
B. Look in the next aisle.
A. Thank you.

* *grandson/granddaughter/. . .*

A. I don't know what to get my
   ....-year-old son/daughter
   for his/her birthday.
B. What about (a) _____?
A. Good idea! Thanks.

A. Mom/Dad? Can we buy
   this/these _____?
B. No, *Johnny*. Not today.

What toys are most popular in your country?

What were your favorite toys when you were
a child?

A make a deposit
B make a withdrawal
C cash a check
D get traveler's checks
E open an account
F apply for a loan
G exchange currency

1 deposit slip
2 withdrawal slip
3 check
4 traveler's check
5 bankbook/passbook
6 ATM card
7 credit card

8 (bank) vault
9 safe deposit box
10 teller
11 security guard
12 ATM (machine)/ cash machine
13 bank officer

[A–G]
A. Where are you going?
B. I'm going to the bank. I have to _____.

[5–7]
A. What are you looking for?
B. My _____. I can't find it anywhere!

[8–13]
A. How many _____s does the State Street Bank have?
B. ....

Do you have a bank account? What kind? Where? What do you do at the bank?

Do you ever use traveler's checks? When?

Do you have a credit card? What kind? When do you use it?

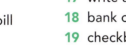

Forms of Payment

1 cash
2 check
  a check number
  b account number
3 credit card
  a credit card number
4 money order
5 traveler's check

Household Bills

6 rent
7 mortgage payment
8 electric bill
9 telephone bill
10 gas bill
11 oil bill/heating bill
12 water bill
13 cable TV bill
14 car payment
15 credit card bill

Family Finances

16 balance the checkbook
17 write a check
18 bank online
19 checkbook
20 check register
21 monthly statement

Using an ATM Machine

22 insert the ATM card
23 enter your PIN number/personal identification number
24 select a transaction
25 make a deposit
26 withdraw/get cash
27 transfer funds
28 remove your card
29 take your transaction slip/receipt

A. Can I pay by ___[1, 2]___/with a ___[3–5]___?
B. Yes. We accept ___[1]___/___[2–5]___s.

A. What are you doing?
B. I'm paying the ___[6–15]___.
  I'm ___[16–18]___ing.
  I'm looking for the ___[19–21]___.

A. What should I do?
B. ___[22–29]___.

What household bills do you receive? How much do you pay for the different bills?

Who takes care of the finances in your household? What does that person do?

Do you use ATM machines? If you do, how do you use them?

1 letter	8 parcel post	16 selective service registration form	24 mail slot
2 postcard	9 certified mail	17 passport application form	25 postal worker/ postal clerk
3 air letter/ aerogramme	10 stamp	18 envelope	26 scale
4 package/parcel	11 sheet of stamps	19 return address	27 stamp machine
5 first class	12 roll of stamps	20 mailing address	28 letter carrier/ mail carrier
6 priority mail	13 book of stamps	21 zip code	29 mail truck
7 express mail/ overnight mail	14 money order	22 postmark	30 mailbox
	15 change-of-address form	23 stamp/postage	

[1–4]
A. Where are you going?
B. To the post office. I have to mail a/an _____ .

[5–9]
A. How do you want to send it?
B. _____ , please.

[10–17]
A. Next!
B. I'd like a _____ , please.
A. Here you are.

[19–21, 23]
A. Do you want me to mail this letter?
B. Yes, thanks.
A. Oops! You forgot the _____ !

How often do you go to the post office? What do you do there?

Tell about the postal system in your country.

1 online catalog
2 card catalog
3 author
4 title
5 library card
6 copier/photocopier/ copy machine
7 shelves
8 children's section
9 children's books

10 periodical section
11 journals
12 magazines
13 newspapers
14 media section
15 books on tape
16 audiotapes
17 CDs
18 videotapes

19 (computer) software
20 DVDs
21 foreign language section
22 foreign language books
23 reference section
24 microfilm
25 microfilm reader

26 dictionary
27 encyclopedia
28 atlas
29 reference desk
30 (reference) librarian
31 checkout desk
32 library clerk

[1, 2, 6–32]
A. Excuse me. Where's/Where are the _____?
B. Over there, at/near/next to the _____.

[8–23, 26–28]
A. Excuse me. Where can I find a/an ___[26–28]___ / ___[9, 11–13, 15–20, 22]___?
B. Look in the ___[8, 10, 14, 21, 23]___ over there.

A. I'm having trouble finding a book.
B. Do you know the ___[3–4]___?
A. Yes. ....

A. Excuse me. I'd like to check out this ___[26–28]___ /these ___[11–13]___.
B. I'm sorry. It/They must remain in the library.

Do you go to a library? Where? What does this library have?

Tell about how you use the library.

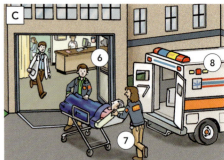

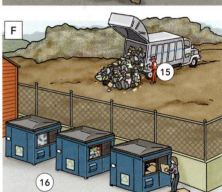

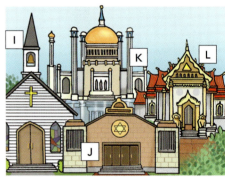

A police station	**I** church	**5** firefighter	**13** game room
B fire station	**J** synagogue	**6** emergency room	**14** swimming pool
C hospital	**K** mosque	**7** EMT/paramedic	**15** sanitation worker
D town hall/city hall	**L** temple	**8** ambulance	**16** recycling center
E recreation center		**9** mayor/city manager	**17** child-care worker
F dump	**1** emergency operator	**10** meeting room	**18** nursery
G child-care center	**2** police officer	**11** gym	**19** playroom
H senior center	**3** police car	**12** activities director	**20** eldercare worker/
	4 fire engine		senior care worker

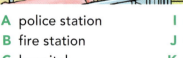

[A–L]
A. Where are you going?
B. I'm going to the _____ .

[1, 2, 5, 7, 12, 15, 17, 20]
A. What do you do?
B. I'm a/an _____ .

[3, 4, 8]
A. Do you hear a siren?
B. Yes. There's a/an _____ coming up behind us.

What community institutions are in your city or town? Where are they located?

Which community institutions do you use? When?

1 car accident	7 kidnapping	13 blackout/power outage	19 vandalism
2 fire	8 lost child	14 gas leak	20 gang violence
3 explosion	9 car jacking	15 water main break	21 drunk driving
4 robbery	10 bank robbery	16 downed power line	22 drug dealing
5 burglary	11 assault	17 chemical spill	
6 mugging	12 murder	18 train derailment	

[1–13]
A. I want to report a/an _____.
B. What's your location?
A. ....

[14–18]
A. Why is this street closed?
B. It's closed because of a _____.

[19–22]
A. I'm very concerned about the amount of _____ in our community.
B. I agree. _____ is a very serious problem.

Is there much crime in your community? Tell about it.

Have you ever experienced a crime or emergency? What happened?

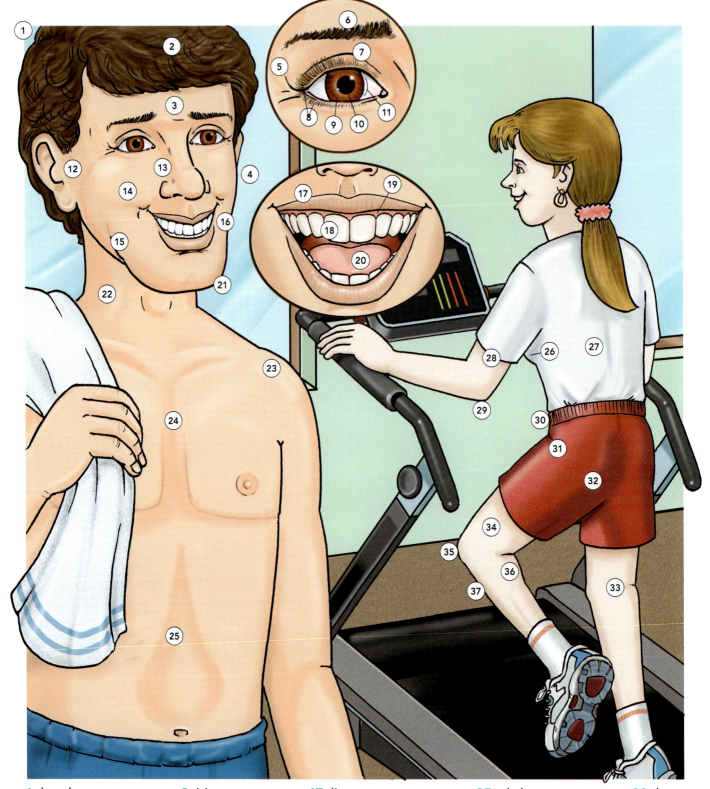

1 head	**9** iris	**17** lip	**25** abdomen	**33** leg
2 hair	**10** pupil	**18** tooth–teeth	**26** breast	**34** thigh
3 forehead	**11** cornea	**19** gums	**27** back	**35** knee
4 face	**12** ear	**20** tongue	**28** arm	**36** calf
5 eye	**13** nose	**21** chin	**29** elbow	**37** shin
6 eyebrow	**14** cheek	**22** neck	**30** waist	
7 eyelid	**15** jaw	**23** shoulder	**31** hip	
8 eyelashes	**16** mouth	**24** chest	**32** buttocks	

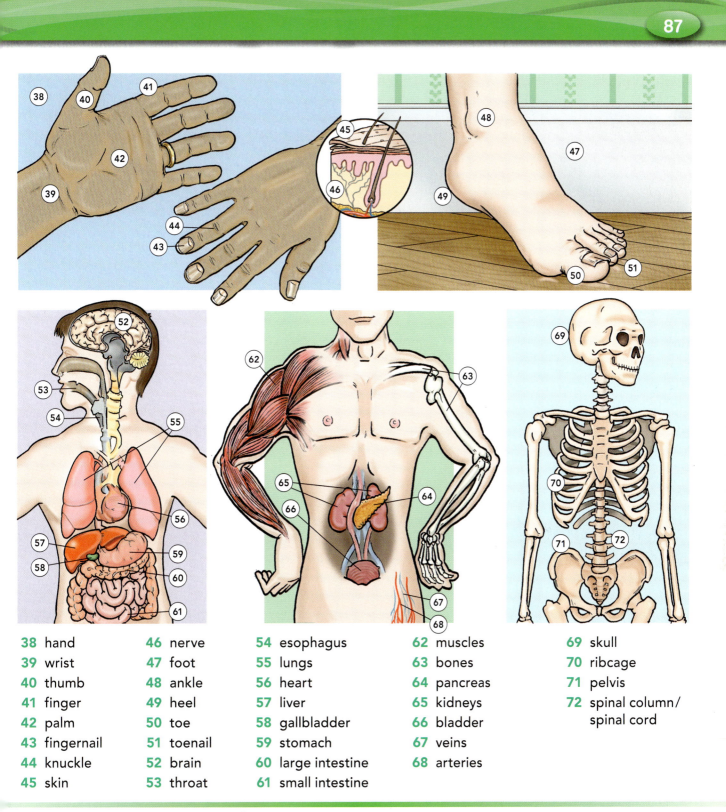

38 hand	46 nerve	54 esophagus	62 muscles	69 skull
39 wrist	47 foot	55 lungs	63 bones	70 ribcage
40 thumb	48 ankle	56 heart	64 pancreas	71 pelvis
41 finger	49 heel	57 liver	65 kidneys	72 spinal column/
42 palm	50 toe	58 gallbladder	66 bladder	spinal cord
43 fingernail	51 toenail	59 stomach	67 veins	
44 knuckle	52 brain	60 large intestine	68 arteries	
45 skin	53 throat	61 small intestine		

A. My doctor checked my **head** and said everything is okay.
B. I'm glad to hear that.

[1, 3–7, 12–29, 31–51]
A. Ooh!
B. What's the matter?
{ My _____ hurts!
{ My _____s hurt!

[52–72]
A. My doctor wants me to have some tests.
B. Why?
A. She's concerned about my _____.

Describe yourself as completely as you can.

Which parts of the body are most important at school? at work? when you play your favorite sport?

1 headache	
2 earache	
3 toothache	
4 stomachache	
5 backache	

6 sore throat	
7 fever/ temperature	
8 cold	
9 cough	
10 infection	

11 rash	
12 insect bite	
13 sunburn	
14 stiff neck	
15 runny nose	
16 bloody nose	

17 cavity	
18 blister	
19 wart	
20 (the) hiccups	
21 (the) chills	

22 cramps	
23 diarrhea	
24 chest pain	
25 shortness of breath	
26 laryngitis	

A. What's the matter?
B. I have a/an _____[1–19]_____.

A. What's the matter?
B. I have _____[20–26]_____.

27 faint	32 exhausted	37 vomit / throw up	42 bruise	46 sprain
28 dizzy	33 cough	38 bleed	43 burn	47 dislocate
29 nauseous	34 sneeze	39 twist	44 hurt–hurt	48 break–broke
30 bloated	35 wheeze	40 scratch	45 cut–cut	49 swollen
31 congested	36 burp	41 scrape		50 itchy

A. What's the problem?
B. { I feel [27–30].
{ I'm [31–32].
{ I've been [33–38]ing a lot.

A. What happened?
B. { I [39–45]ed my ....
{ I think I [46–48]ed my ....
{ My .... is / are [49–50].

A. How do you feel?
B. Not so good. / Not very well. / Terrible!
A. What's the matter?
B. ...., ..., and ....
A. I'm sorry to hear that.

Tell about the last time you didn't feel well. What was the matter?

Tell about a time you hurt yourself. What happened? How? What did you do about it?

What do you do when you have a cold? a stomachache? an insect bite? the hiccups?

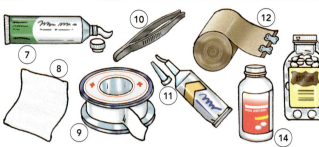
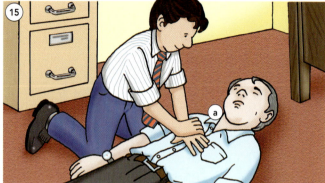

1 first-aid manual	8 gauze
2 first-aid kit	9 adhesive tape
3 (adhesive) bandage/ Band-Aid™	10 tweezers
4 antiseptic cleansing wipe	11 antihistamine cream
5 sterile (dressing) pad	12 elastic bandage/ Ace™ bandage
6 hydrogen peroxide	13 aspirin
7 antibiotic ointment	14 non-aspirin pain reliever

15 CPR (cardiopulmonary resuscitation)	18 splint
a has no pulse	d broke a finger
16 rescue breathing	19 tourniquet
b isn't breathing	e is bleeding
17 the Heimlich maneuver	
c is choking	

A. Do we have any ___[3–5, 12]___s/ ___[6–11, 13, 14]___?
B. Yes. Look in the first-aid kit.

A. Help! My friend ___[a–e]___!
B. I can help!
{ I know how to do ___[15–17]___.
{ I can make a ___[18, 19]___.

Do you have a first-aid kit? If you do, what's in it? If you don't, where can you buy one?

Tell about a time when you gave or received first aid.

Where can a person learn first aid in your community?

1 hurt / injured
2 in shock
3 unconscious
4 heatstroke
5 frostbite

6 heart attack
7 allergic reaction
8 swallow poison
9 overdose on drugs
10 fall–fell

11 get–got an electric shock
12 the flu / influenza
13 an ear infection
14 strep throat
15 measles

16 mumps
17 chicken pox
18 asthma
19 cancer
20 depression

21 diabetes
22 heart disease
23 high blood pressure / hypertension
24 TB / tuberculosis
25 AIDS*

* Acquired Immune Deficiency Syndrome

A. What happened?
B. My ....
  is _____[1–3]_____.
  has _____[4–5]_____.
  is having a/an _____[6–7]_____.
  _____[8–11]_____ ed.
A. What's your location?
B. ....(address)...........

A. My .... is sick.
B. What's the matter?
A. He/She has _____[12–25]_____.
B. I'm sorry to hear that.

Tell about a medical emergency that happened to you or someone you know.

Which illnesses in this lesson are you familiar with?

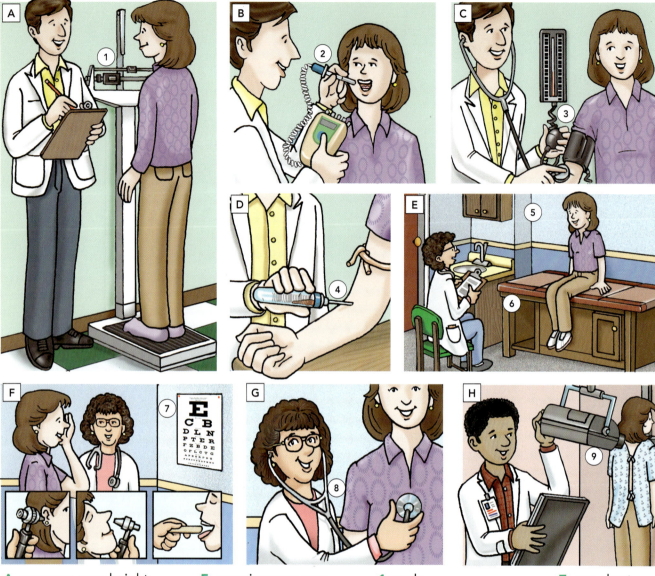

A measure *your* height and weight

B take *your* temperature

C check *your* blood pressure

D draw some blood

E ask *you* some questions about *your* health

F examine *your* eyes, ears, nose, and throat

G listen to *your* heart

H take a chest X-ray

1 scale

2 thermometer

3 blood pressure gauge

4 needle/syringe

5 examination room

6 examination table

7 eye chart

8 stethoscope

9 X-ray machine

[A–H]

A. Now I'm going to **measure your height and weight**.

B. All right.

[A–H]

A. What did the doctor/nurse do during the examination?

B. She/He **measured my height and weight**.

[1–3, 5–9]

A. So, how do you like our new **scale**?

B. It's very nice, doctor.

How often do you have a medical exam?

What does the doctor/nurse do?

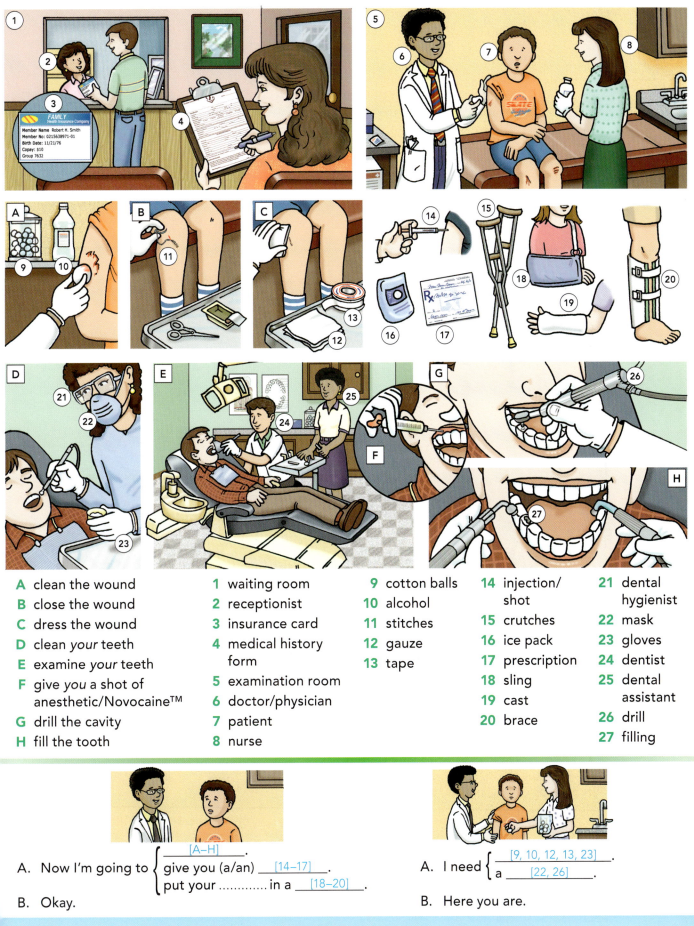

A clean the wound
B close the wound
C dress the wound
D clean *your* teeth
E examine *your* teeth
F give *you* a shot of anesthetic/Novocaine™
G drill the cavity
H fill the tooth

1 waiting room
2 receptionist
3 insurance card
4 medical history form
5 examination room
6 doctor/physician
7 patient
8 nurse

9 cotton balls
10 alcohol
11 stitches
12 gauze
13 tape

14 injection/ shot
15 crutches
16 ice pack
17 prescription
18 sling
19 cast
20 brace

21 dental hygienist
22 mask
23 gloves
24 dentist
25 dental assistant
26 drill
27 filling

A. Now I'm going to { ____[A–H]____.
give you (a/an) ____[14–17]____.
put your .... in a ____[18–20]____.

B. Okay.

A. I need { ____[9, 10, 12, 13, 23]____.
a ____[22, 26]____.

B. Here you are.

Tell about a personal experience you had with a medical or dental procedure.

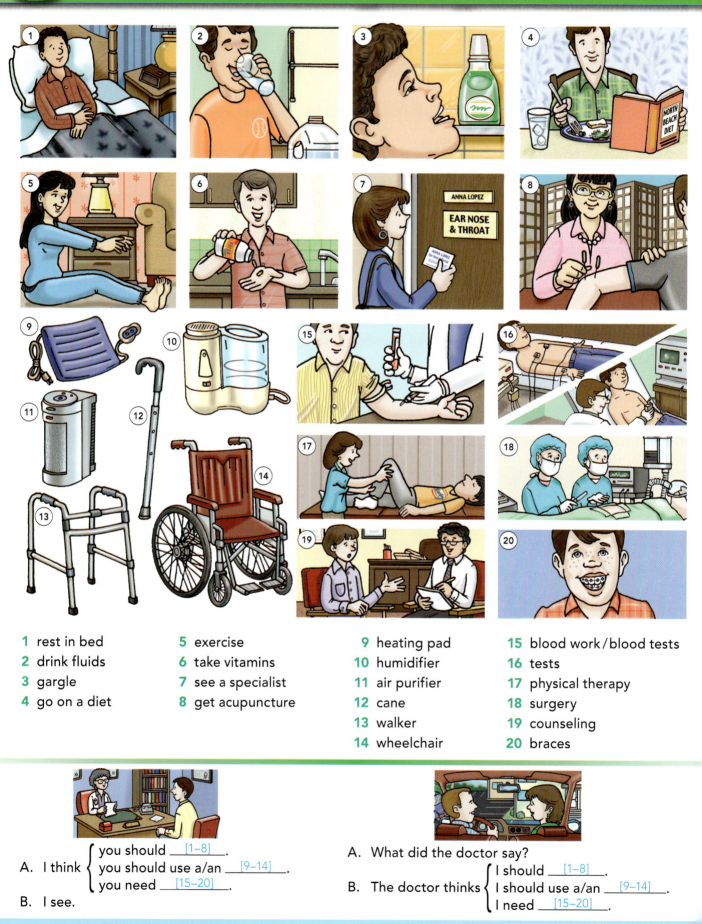

1 rest in bed
2 drink fluids
3 gargle
4 go on a diet

5 exercise
6 take vitamins
7 see a specialist
8 get acupuncture

9 heating pad
10 humidifier
11 air purifier
12 cane
13 walker
14 wheelchair

15 blood work / blood tests
16 tests
17 physical therapy
18 surgery
19 counseling
20 braces

A. I think { you should _____[1–8]_____.
               you should use a/an _____[9–14]_____.
               you need _____[15–20]_____.

B. I see.

A. What did the doctor say?

B. The doctor thinks { I should _____[1–8]_____.
                        I should use a/an _____[9–14]_____.
                        I need _____[15–20]_____.

Tell about medical advice a doctor gave you.
What did the doctor say? Did you follow the advice?

1 aspirin
2 cold tablets
3 vitamins
4 cough syrup
5 non-aspirin pain
   reliever

6 cough drops
7 throat lozenges
8 antacid tablets
9 decongestant spray/
   nasal spray

10 eye drops
11 ointment
12 cream/creme
13 lotion

14 pill
15 tablet
16 capsule
17 caplet
18 teaspoon
19 tablespoon

[1–13]
A. What did the doctor say?
B. { She/He told me to take _____[1–4]_____/a ___[5]___.
    { She/He told me to use _____[6–13]_____.

[14–19]
A. What's the dosage?
B. One _____ every four hours.

What medicines in this lesson do you have at home? What other medicines do you have?

What do you take or use for a fever? a headache? a stomachache? a sore throat? a cold? a cough?

Tell about any medicines in your country that are different from the ones in this lesson.

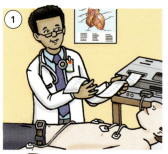

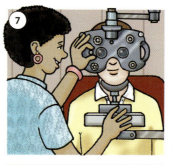

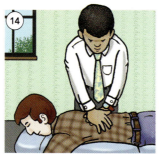

1 cardiologist	5 allergist	9 audiologist	13 gastroenterologist
2 gynecologist	6 orthopedist	10 physical therapist	14 chiropractor
3 pediatrician	7 ophthalmologist	11 counselor/therapist	15 acupuncturist
4 gerontologist	8 ear, nose, and throat (ENT) specialist	12 psychiatrist	16 orthodontist

A. I think you need to see a specialist.
   I'm going to refer you to a/an _____.
B. A/An _____?
A. Yes.

A. When is your next appointment with the _____?
B. It's at ....(time).......... on ....(date)...........

Do you or members of your family see any of these medical specialists? Which ones?

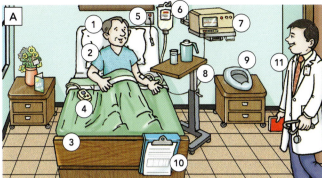

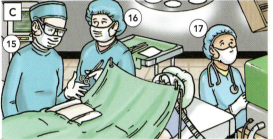

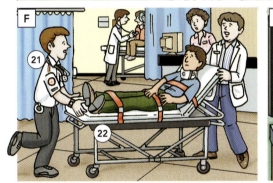

A patient's room
1 patient
2 hospital gown
3 hospital bed
4 bed control
5 call button
6 I.V.
7 vital signs monitor
8 bed table
9 bed pan
10 medical chart
11 doctor/physician

B nurse's station
12 nurse
13 dietitian
14 orderly

C operating room
15 surgeon
16 surgical nurse
17 anesthesiologist

D waiting room
18 volunteer

**E birthing room/
delivery room**
19 obstetrician
20 midwife/nurse-midwife

F emergency room/ER
21 emergency medical
technician/EMT
22 gurney

G radiology department
23 X-ray technician
24 radiologist

H laboratory/lab
25 lab technician

A. This is your _____[2–10]_____.
B. I see.

A. Do you work here?
B. Yes. I'm a/an _____[11–21, 23–25]_____.

A. Where's the _____[11–21, 23–25]_____?

B. She's/He's { in the _____[A, C–H]_____.
             at the _____[B]_____.

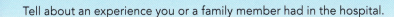

Tell about an experience you or a family member had in the hospital.

A **brush** *my* **teeth**
1 toothbrush
2 toothpaste

B **floss** *my* **teeth**
3 dental floss

C **gargle**
4 mouthwash

D **whiten** *my* **teeth**
5 teeth whitener

E **bathe / take a bath**
6 soap
7 bubble bath

F **take a shower**
8 shower cap

G **wash** *my* **hair**
9 shampoo
10 conditioner / rinse

H **dry** *my* **hair**
11 hair dryer / blow dryer

I **comb** *my* **hair**
12 comb

J **brush** *my* **hair**
13 (hair) brush

K **style** *my* **hair**
14 hot comb / curling iron
15 hairspray
16 hair gel
17 bobby pin
18 barrette
19 hairclip

L shave	28 nail clipper	37 cologne/perfume
20 shaving cream	29 nail brush	38 sunscreen
21 razor	30 scissors	
22 razor blade	31 nail polish	**O put on makeup**
23 electric shaver	32 nail polish remover	39 blush/rouge
24 styptic pencil		40 foundation/base
25 aftershave (lotion)	**N put on . . .**	41 moisturizer
	33 deodorant	42 face powder
M do my nails	34 hand lotion	43 eyeliner
26 nail file	35 body lotion	
27 emery board	36 powder	

44 eye shadow
45 mascara
46 eyebrow pencil
47 lipstick

P polish my shoes
48 shoe polish
49 shoelaces

[A–M, N (33–38), O, P]
A. What are you doing?
B. I'm _____ing.

[1, 8, 11–14, 17–19, 21–24, 26–30, 46, 49]
A. Excuse me. Where can I find _____(s)?
B. They're in the next aisle.

[2–7, 9, 10, 15, 16, 20, 25, 31–45, 47, 48]
A. Excuse me. Where can I find _____?
B. It's in the next aisle.

Which of these personal care products do you use?

You're going on a trip. Make a list of the personal care products you need to take with you.

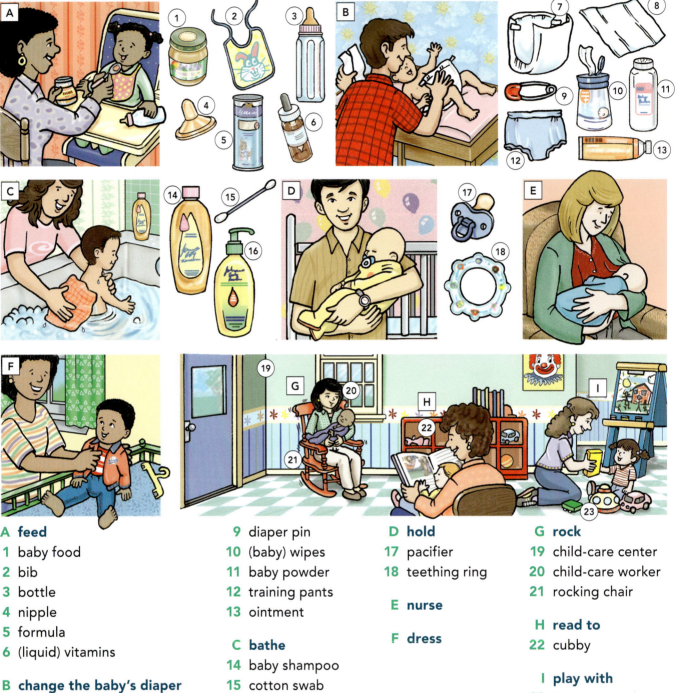

A feed
1 baby food
2 bib
3 bottle
4 nipple
5 formula
6 (liquid) vitamins

B change the baby's diaper
7 disposable diaper
8 cloth diaper

9 diaper pin
10 (baby) wipes
11 baby powder
12 training pants
13 ointment

C bathe
14 baby shampoo
15 cotton swab
16 baby lotion

D hold
17 pacifier
18 teething ring

E nurse

F dress

G rock
19 child-care center
20 child-care worker
21 rocking chair

H read to
22 cubby

I play with
23 toys

A. What are you doing?
B. { I'm _____[A, C–I]_____ing the baby.
     I'm _____[B]_____ing.

A. Do we need anything from the store?
B. Yes. We need some more { _____[2–4, 7–9, 15, 17, 18]_____s
                              _____[1, 5, 6, 10–14, 16]_____.

In your opinion, which are better: cloth diapers or disposable diapers? Why?

Tell about baby products in your country.

1 preschool/nursery school
2 elementary school
3 middle school/junior high school
4 high school

5 adult school
6 vocational school/trade school
7 community college
8 college

9 university
10 graduate school
11 law school
12 medical school

A. Are you a student?
B. Yes. I'm in _____[1–4, 8, 10–12]_____.

A. Are you a student?
B. Yes. I go to a/an _____[5–7, 9]_____.

A. Is this apartment building near a/an _____?
B. Yes. _____(name of school)_____ is nearby.

A. Tell me about your previous education.
B. I went to _____(name of school)_____.
A. Did you like it there?
B. Yes. It was an excellent _____.

What types of schools are there in your community? What are their names, and where are they located?

What types of schools have you gone to?

Where? When? What did you study?

A (main) office	**H** gym / gymnasium	**1** clerk / (school) secretary	**8** science teacher
B principal's office	**a** locker room	**2** principal	**9** P.E. teacher
C nurse's office	**I** track	**3** (school) nurse	**10** coach
D guidance office	**a** bleachers	**4** (guidance) counselor	**11** custodian
E classroom	**J** field	**5** teacher	**12** cafeteria worker
F hallway	**K** auditorium	**6** assistant principal /	**13** lunchroom monitor
a locker	**L** cafeteria	vice-principal	**14** (school) librarian
G science lab	**M** library	**7** security officer	

A. Where are you going?
B. I'm going to the ____[A–D, G–M]____ .
A. Do you have a hall pass?
B. Yes. Here it is.

A. Where's the ____[1–14]____ ?
B. He's / She's in the ____[A–M]____ .

Describe the school where you study English. Tell about the rooms, offices, and people.

Tell about differences between the school in this lesson and schools in your country.

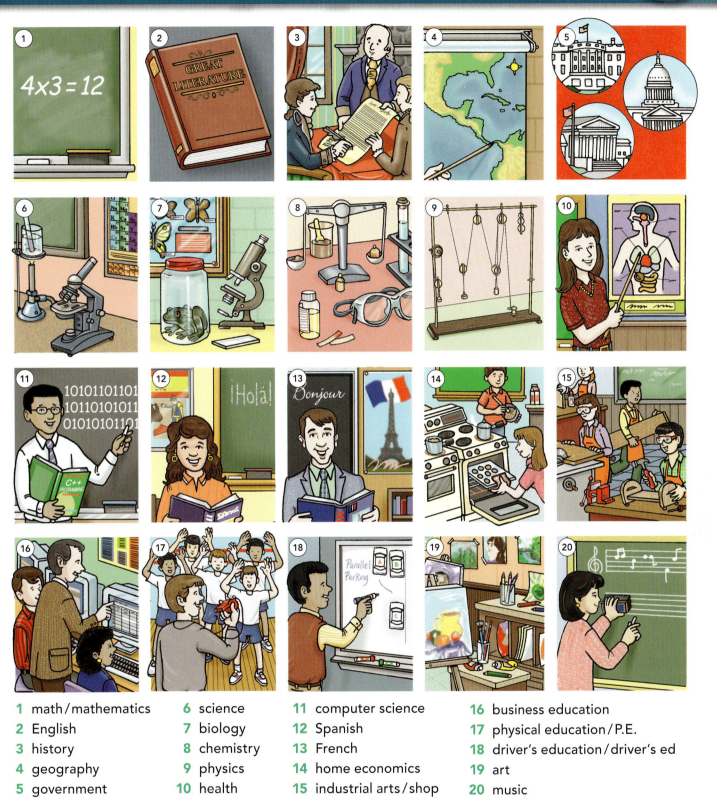

1 math / mathematics
2 English
3 history
4 geography
5 government
6 science
7 biology
8 chemistry
9 physics
10 health
11 computer science
12 Spanish
13 French
14 home economics
15 industrial arts / shop
16 business education
17 physical education / P.E.
18 driver's education / driver's ed
19 art
20 music

A. What do you have next period?
B. **Math**. How about you?
A. **English**.
B. There's the bell. I've got to go.

What is/was your favorite subject? Why?

In your opinion, what's the most interesting subject? the most difficult subject? Why do you think so?

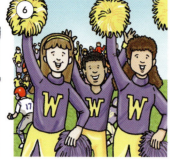

1 band	**5** football	**9** school newspaper	**13** debate club
2 orchestra	**6** cheerleading/pep squad	**10** yearbook	**14** computer club
3 choir/chorus	**7** student government	**11** literary magazine	**15** international club
4 drama	**8** community service	**12** A.V. crew	**16** chess club

A. Are you going home right after school?

B. {
  No. I have _____[1–6]_____ practice.
  No. I have a _____[7–16]_____ meeting.

What extracurricular activities do/did you participate in?

Which extracurricular activities in this lesson are there in schools in your country? What other activities are there?

Arithmetic

$$2+1=3 \qquad 8-3=5 \qquad 4\times2=8 \qquad 10\div2=5$$

addition	subtraction	multiplication	division
2 **plus** 1 **equals*** 3.	8 **minus** 3 **equals*** 5.	4 **times** 2 **equals*** 8.	10 **divided by** 2 **equals*** 5.

You can also say: **is**

A. How much is *two plus one?*
B. *Two plus one* equals/is *three.*

Make conversations for the arithmetic problems above and others.

Fractions

1/4	1/3	1/2	2/3	3/4
one quarter/ one fourth	one third	one half/ half	two thirds	three quarters/ three fourths

A. Is this on sale?
B. Yes. It's _____ off the regular price.

A. Is the gas tank almost empty?
B. It's about _____ full.

Percents

10% ten percent	50% fifty percent	75% seventy-five percent	100% one-hundred percent

A. How did you do on the test?
B. I got _____ percent of the answers right.

A. What's the weather forecast?
B. There's a _____ percent chance of rain.

Types of Math

$5y-5y+3=$		$\sin(y)=x$	$\int_{2}^{6} g(x)\,dx$	
algebra	geometry	trigonometry	calculus	statistics

A. What math course are you taking this year?
B. I'm taking _____.

Are you good at math?

What math courses do/did you take in school?

Tell about something you bought on sale. How much off the regular price was it?

Research and discuss: What percentage of people in your country live in cities? live on farms? work in factories? vote in general elections?

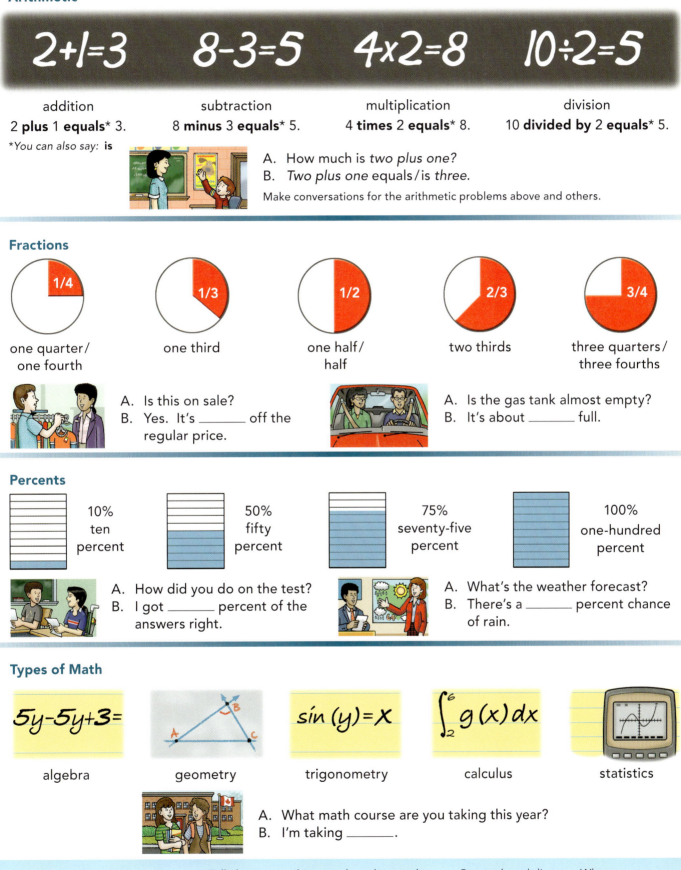

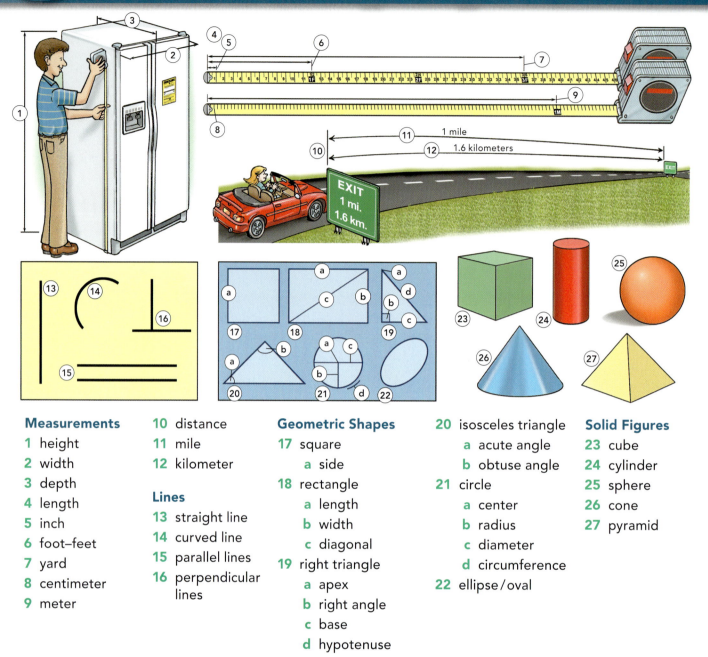

Measurements

1 height
2 width
3 depth
4 length
5 inch
6 foot–feet
7 yard
8 centimeter
9 meter
10 distance
11 mile
12 kilometer

Lines

13 straight line
14 curved line
15 parallel lines
16 perpendicular lines

Geometric Shapes

17 square
   a side
18 rectangle
   a length
   b width
   c diagonal
19 right triangle
   a apex
   b right angle
   c base
   d hypotenuse
20 isosceles triangle
   a acute angle
   b obtuse angle
21 circle
   a center
   b radius
   c diameter
   d circumference
22 ellipse/oval

Solid Figures

23 cube
24 cylinder
25 sphere
26 cone
27 pyramid

[1–9]
A. What's the ___[1–4]___ ?
B. .... ___[5–9]___ (s).

[11–12]
A. What's the distance?
B. .... _____ (s).

1 inch (1") = 2.54 centimeters (cm)
1 foot (1') = 0.305 meters (m)
1 yard (1 yd.) = 0.914 meters (m)
1 mile (mi.) = 1.6 kilometers (km)

[17–22]
A. Who can tell me what shape this is?
B. I can. It's a/an _____ .

[23–27]
A. Who knows what figure this is?
B. I do. It's a/an _____ .

[13–27]
A. This painting is magnificent!
B. Hmm. I don't think so. It just looks like a lot of _____ s and _____ s to me!

Types of Sentences & Parts of Speech

A **Students study in the new library.** ① ② ③ ④ ⑤

C **Read page nine.**

B **Do they study hard?** ⑥ ⑦

D **This cake is fantastic!**

A declarative
B interrogative
C imperative
D exclamatory

1 noun
2 verb
3 preposition
4 article

5 adjective
6 pronoun
7 adverb

A. What type of sentence is this?
B. It's a/an ___[A–D]___ sentence.

A. What part of speech is this?
B. It's a/an ___[1–7]___.

Punctuation Marks & the Writing Process

8 period
9 question mark
10 exclamation point
11 comma

12 apostrophe
13 quotation marks
14 colon
15 semi-colon

16 brainstorm ideas
17 organize *my* ideas
18 write a first draft
 a title
 b paragraph

19 make corrections/ revise/edit
20 get feedback
21 write a final copy/ rewrite

A. Did you find any mistakes?
B. Yes. You forgot to put a/an ___[8–15]___ in this sentence.

A. Are you working on your composition?
B. Yes. I'm ___[16–21]___ing.

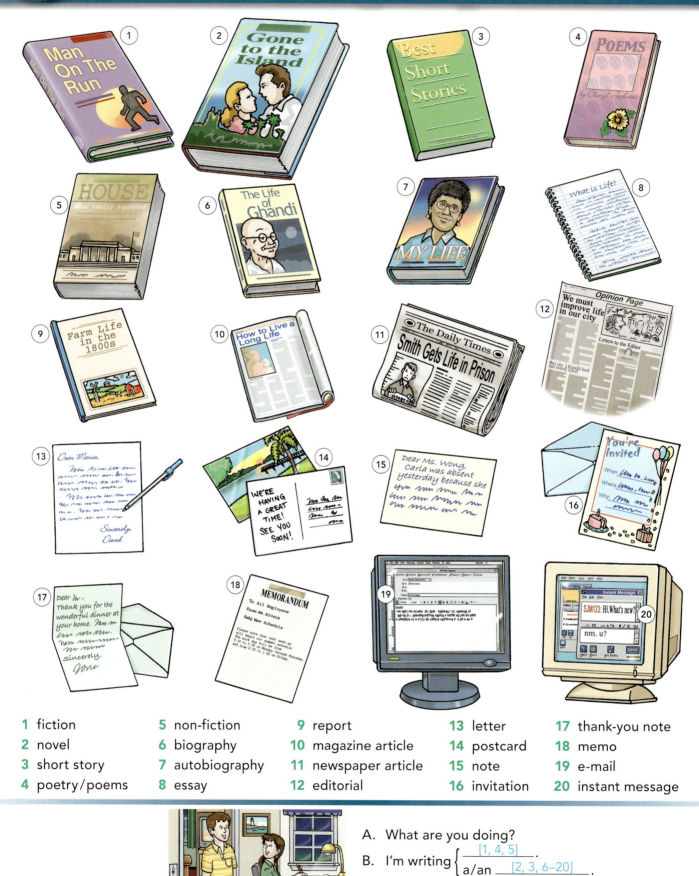

1 fiction
2 novel
3 short story
4 poetry / poems

5 non-fiction
6 biography
7 autobiography
8 essay

9 report
10 magazine article
11 newspaper article
12 editorial

13 letter
14 postcard
15 note
16 invitation

17 thank-you note
18 memo
19 e-mail
20 instant message

A. What are you doing?
B. I'm writing { _____[1, 4, 5]_____.
        a/an _____[2, 3, 6–20]_____.

What kind of literature do you like to read? What are some of your favorite books? Who is your favorite author?

Do you like to read newspapers and magazines? Which ones do you read?

Do you sometimes send or receive letters, postcards, notes, e-mail, or instant messages? Tell about the people you communicate with, and how.

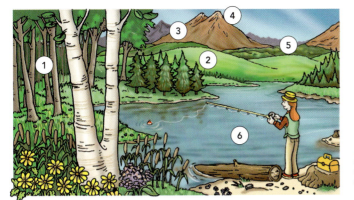

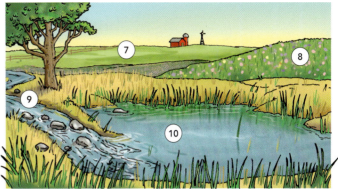

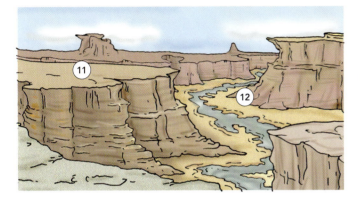

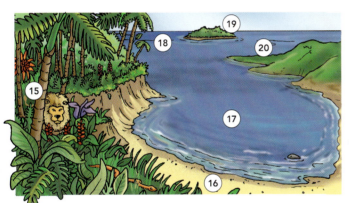

1 forest/woods	**7** plains	**13** dune/sand dune	**19** island
2 hill	**8** meadow	**14** desert	**20** peninsula
3 mountain range	**9** stream/brook	**15** jungle	**21** rainforest
4 mountain peak	**10** pond	**16** seashore/shore	**22** river
5 valley	**11** plateau	**17** bay	**23** waterfall
6 lake	**12** canyon	**18** ocean	

A. { Isn't this a beautiful _____?!
{ Aren't these beautiful _____s?!

B. Yes. It's/They're magnificent!

Tell about the geography of your country. Describe the different geographic features.

Have you seen some of the geographic features in this lesson? Which ones? Where?

Science Equipment

1 microscope
2 computer
3 slide
4 Petri dish
5 flask
6 funnel
7 beaker
8 test tube
9 forceps
10 crucible tongs
11 Bunsen burner
12 graduated cylinder
13 magnet
14 prism
15 dropper
16 chemicals
17 balance
18 scale

The Scientific Method

A state the problem
B form a hypothesis
C plan a procedure
D do a procedure
E make/record observations
F draw conclusions

A. What do we need to do this procedure?
B. We need a/an/the ___[1–18]___.

A. How is your experiment coming along?
B. I'm getting ready to ___[A–F]___.

Do you have experience with the scientific equipment in this lesson? Tell about it.

What science courses do/did you take in school?

Think of an idea for a science experiment.
What question about science do you want to answer? State the problem.
What do you think will happen in the experiment? Form a hypothesis.
How can you test your hypothesis? Plan a procedure.

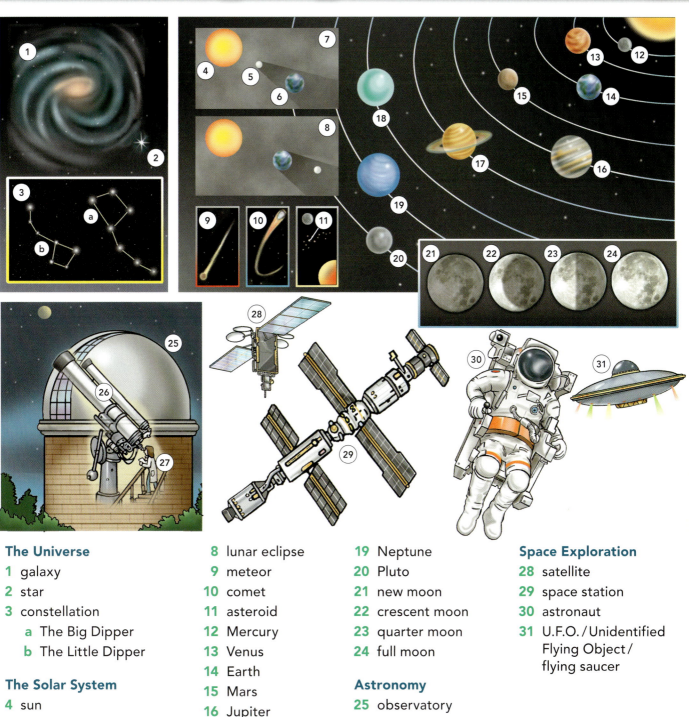

The Universe

1 galaxy
2 star
3 constellation
  a The Big Dipper
  b The Little Dipper

The Solar System

4 sun
5 moon
6 planet
7 solar eclipse
8 lunar eclipse
9 meteor
10 comet
11 asteroid
12 Mercury
13 Venus
14 Earth
15 Mars
16 Jupiter
17 Saturn
18 Uranus
19 Neptune
20 Pluto
21 new moon
22 crescent moon
23 quarter moon
24 full moon

Astronomy

25 observatory
26 telescope
27 astronomer

Space Exploration

28 satellite
29 space station
30 astronaut
31 U.F.O. / Unidentified
  Flying Object /
  flying saucer

[1–24]
A. Is that (a/an/the) _____?
B. I'm not sure. I think it might be
  (a/an/the) _____.

[28–30]
A. Is the _____ ready for
  tomorrow's launch?
B. Yes. "All systems are go!"

Pretend you are an astronaut traveling in space.
What do you see?

Draw and name a constellation you are familiar with.

Do you think space exploration is important? Why?

Have you ever seen a U.F.O.? Do you believe there
is life in outer space? Why?

1	accountant	6	assembler	10	bricklayer/mason	15	cashier	19	construction worker
2	actor	7	babysitter	11	businessman	16	chef/cook	20	custodian/janitor
3	actress	8	baker	12	businesswoman	17	child day-care worker	21	customer service representative
4	architect	9	barber	13	butcher	18	computer software engineer	22	data entry clerk
5	artist			14	carpenter				

23 delivery person
24 dockworker
25 engineer
26 factory worker

27 farmer
28 firefighter
29 fisher
30 food-service worker

31 foreman
32 gardener/landscaper
33 garment worker
34 hairdresser

35 health-care aide/attendant
36 home health aide/ home attendant
37 homemaker
38 housekeeper

A. What do you do?
B. I'm an **accountant**. How about you?
A. I'm a **carpenter**.

[At a job interview]
A. Are you an experienced _____?
B. Yes. I'm a very experienced _____.

A. How long have you been a/an _____?
B. I've been a/an _____ for .... months/years.

Which of these occupations do you think are the most interesting? the most difficult? Why?

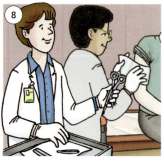

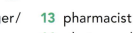

1 journalist/reporter
2 lawyer
3 machine operator
4 mail carrier/
letter carrier

5 manager
6 manicurist
7 mechanic
8 medical assistant/
physician assistant

9 messenger/
courier
10 mover
11 musician
12 painter

13 pharmacist
14 photographer
15 pilot
16 police officer

17 postal worker
18 receptionist
19 repairperson
20 salesperson

21 sanitation worker / trash collector
22 secretary
23 security guard
24 serviceman
25 servicewoman

26 stock clerk
27 store owner / shopkeeper
28 supervisor
29 tailor

30 teacher / instructor
31 telemarketer
32 translator / interpreter
33 travel agent

34 truck driver
35 veterinarian / vet
36 waiter / server
37 waitress / server
38 welder

A. What's your occupation?
B. I'm a **journalist**.
A. A **journalist**?
B. Yes. That's right.

A. Are you still a _____?
B. No. I'm a _____.
A. Oh. That's interesting.

A. What kind of job would you like in the future?
B. I'd like to be a _____.

Do you work? What's your occupation?

What are the occupations of people in your family?

JOB SKILLS AND ACTIVITIES

1 act
2 assemble components
3 assist *patients*
4 bake
5 build *things* / construct *things*
6 clean
7 cook
8 deliver *pizzas*
9 design *buildings*
10 draw
11 drive *a truck*
12 file
13 fly *an airplane*
14 grow *vegetables*
15 guard *buildings*
16 manage *a restaurant*
17 mow *lawns*
18 operate *equipment*
19 paint
20 play the *piano*

21 prepare *food*
22 repair *things* / fix *things*
23 sell *cars*
24 serve *food*

25 sew
26 sing
27 speak *Spanish*
28 supervise *people*

29 take care of *elderly people*
30 take inventory
31 teach
32 translate

33 type
34 use *a cash register*
35 wash *dishes*
36 write

A. Can you **act**?
B. Yes, I can.

A. Do you know how to _____?
B. Yes. I've been _____ing for years.

A. Tell me about your skills.
B. I can _____, and I can _____.

Tell about your job skills.
What can you do?

Types of Job Ads

1 help wanted sign
2 job notice / job announcement
3 classified ad / want ad

Job Ad Abbreviations

4 full-time
5 part-time
6 available
7 hour
8 Monday through Friday
9 evenings
10 previous
11 experience
12 required
13 excellent

Job Search

A respond to an ad
B request information
C request an interview
D prepare a resume
E dress appropriately
F fill out an application (form)
G go to an interview
H talk about your skills and qualifications
I talk about your experience
J ask about the salary
K ask about the benefits
L write a thank-you note
M get hired

A. How did you find your job?
B. I found it through a _____[1–3]_____.

A. How was your job interview?
B. It went very well.
A. Did you _____[D–F, H–M]_____?
B. Yes, I did.

Tell about a job you are familiar with. What are the skills and qualifications required for the job? What are the hours? What is the salary?

Tell about how people you know found their jobs.

Tell about your own experience with a job search or a job interview.

A reception area	**1** coat rack	**11** swivel chair	**21** employer/boss	**a** take a message
B conference room	**2** coat closet	**12** typewriter	**22** administrative assistant	**b** give a presentation
C mailroom	**3** receptionist	**13** adding machine	**23** office manager	**c** sort the mail
D work area	**4** conference table	**14** copier/photocopier	**24** supply cabinet	**d** make copies
E office	**5** presentation board	**15** paper shredder	**25** storage cabinet	**e** file
F supply room	**6** postal scale	**16** paper cutter	**26** vending machine	**f** type a letter
G storage room	**7** postage meter	**17** file clerk	**27** water cooler	
H employee lounge	**8** office assistant	**18** file cabinet	**28** coffee machine	
	9 mailbox	**19** secretary	**29** message board	
	10 cubicle	**20** computer workstation		

[A–H]
A. Where's ....(name)....?
B. He's/She's in the _____.

[1–29]
A. What do you think of the new _____?
B. He's/She's/It's very nice.

[a–f]
A. What's ....(name).... doing?
B. He's/She's _____ing.

Describe a workplace you are familiar with.
Tell about the rooms, the areas, and the employees.

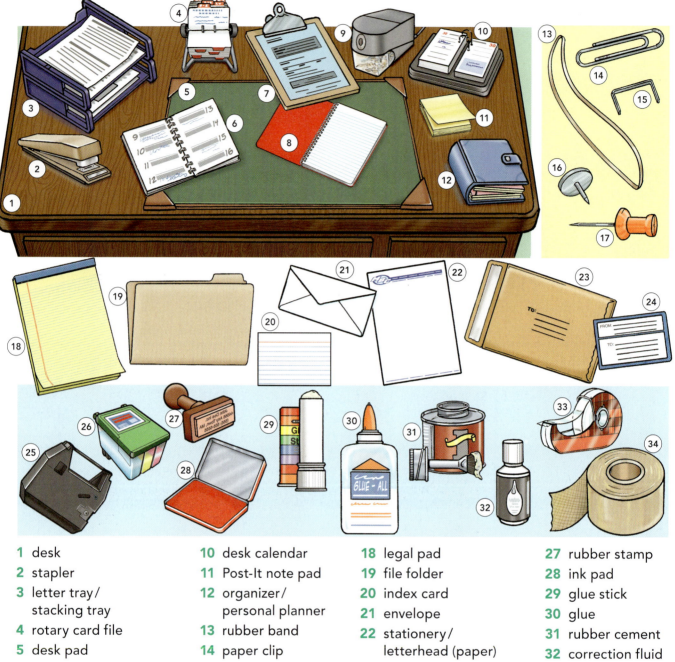

1 desk
2 stapler
3 letter tray /
   stacking tray
4 rotary card file
5 desk pad
6 appointment book
7 clipboard
8 note pad / memo pad
9 electric pencil
   sharpener

10 desk calendar
11 Post-It note pad
12 organizer /
   personal planner
13 rubber band
14 paper clip
15 staple
16 thumbtack
17 pushpin

18 legal pad
19 file folder
20 index card
21 envelope
22 stationery /
   letterhead (paper)
23 mailer
24 mailing label
25 typewriter cartridge
26 ink cartridge

27 rubber stamp
28 ink pad
29 glue stick
30 glue
31 rubber cement
32 correction fluid
33 cellophane tape /
   clear tape
34 packing tape /
   sealing tape

A. My desk is a mess!
   I can't find my __[2–12]__ !
B. Here it is next to your __[2–12]__ .

A. Could you get some more
   __[13–21, 23–29]__ s / __[22, 30–34]__
   from the supply room?
B. Some more __[13–21, 23–29]__ s /
   __[22, 30–34]__ ? Sure. I'd be happy to.

Which supplies and equipment do you use? What do you use them for?

Which supplies in this lesson do you have at home? at school?

1	time clock	7	line supervisor	13	forklift	18	shipping clerk
2	time cards	8	quality control supervisor	14	freight elevator	19	hand truck / dolly
3	locker room	9	machine	15	union notice	20	loading dock
4	(assembly) line	10	conveyor belt	16	suggestion box	21	payroll office
5	(factory) worker	11	warehouse	17	shipping department	22	personnel office
6	work station	12	packer				

A. Excuse me. I'm a new employee.
   Where's / Where are the _____?
B. Next to / Near / In / On the _____.

A. Have you seen *Tony*?
B. Yes. *He's* in / on / at / next to / near
   the _____.

Are there any factories where you live? What kind? What are the working conditions there?

What products do factories in your country produce?

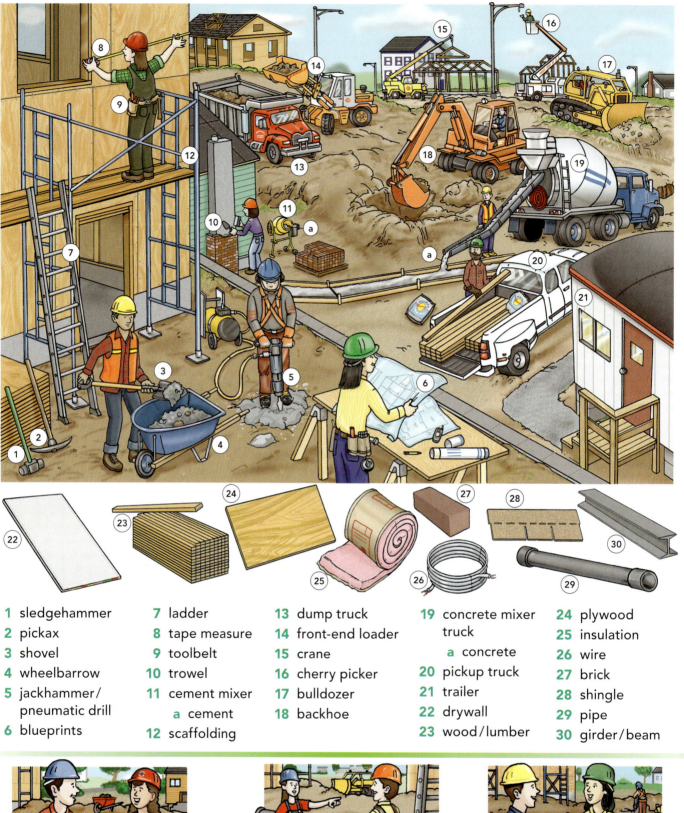

1 sledgehammer	**7** ladder	**13** dump truck	**19** concrete mixer truck	**24** plywood
2 pickax	**8** tape measure	**14** front-end loader	**a** concrete	**25** insulation
3 shovel	**9** toolbelt	**15** crane	**20** pickup truck	**26** wire
4 wheelbarrow	**10** trowel	**16** cherry picker	**21** trailer	**27** brick
5 jackhammer / pneumatic drill	**11** cement mixer	**17** bulldozer	**22** drywall	**28** shingle
6 blueprints	**a** cement	**18** backhoe	**23** wood / lumber	**29** pipe
	12 scaffolding			**30** girder / beam

A. Could you get me that / those ___[1–10]___ ?
B. Sure.

A. Watch out for that ___[11–21]___ !
B. Oh! Thanks for the warning!

A. Do we have enough ___[22–26]___ / ___[27–30]___ s?
B. I think so.

What building materials is your home made of? When was it built?

Describe a construction site near your home or school. Tell about the construction equipment and the materials.

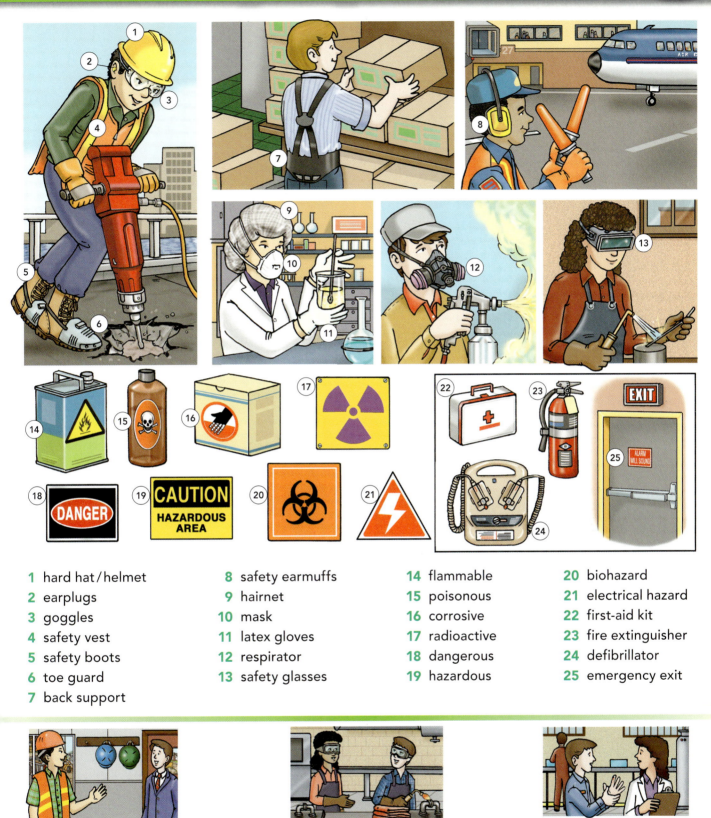

1 hard hat / helmet
2 earplugs
3 goggles
4 safety vest
5 safety boots
6 toe guard
7 back support

8 safety earmuffs
9 hairnet
10 mask
11 latex gloves
12 respirator
13 safety glasses

14 flammable
15 poisonous
16 corrosive
17 radioactive
18 dangerous
19 hazardous

20 biohazard
21 electrical hazard
22 first-aid kit
23 fire extinguisher
24 defibrillator
25 emergency exit

A. Don't forget to wear your ___[1–13]___!
B. Thanks for reminding me.

A. Be careful!
{
That material is ___[14–17]___!
That machine is ___[18]___!
That work area is ___[19]___!
That's a ___[20]___! / That's an ___[21]___!
}
B. Thanks for the warning.

A. Where's the ___[22–25]___?
B. It's over there.

Have you ever used any of the safety equipment in this lesson? What have you used? When? Where?

Where do you see people using safety equipment in your community?

A bus
1 bus stop
2 bus route
3 passenger / rider
4 (bus) fare
5 transfer
6 bus driver
7 bus station
8 ticket counter

9 ticket
10 baggage compartment /
   luggage compartment

B train
11 train station
12 ticket window
13 arrival and departure
   board
14 information booth

15 schedule / timetable
16 platform
17 track
18 conductor

C subway
19 subway station
20 (subway) token
21 turnstile
22 fare card

23 fare card machine

D taxi
24 taxi stand
25 taxi / cab / taxicab
26 meter
27 cab driver / taxi driver

E ferry

[A–E]
A. How are you going to get there?
B. ⎰ I'm going to take the ___[A–C, E]___ .
   ⎱ I'm going to take a ___[D]___ .

[1, 7, 8, 10–19, 21, 23–25]
A. Excuse me. Where's the _____?
B. Over there.

How do you get to different places in your community?
Describe public transportation where you live.

In your country, can you travel far by train or by bus? Where can
you go? How much do tickets cost? Describe the buses and trains.

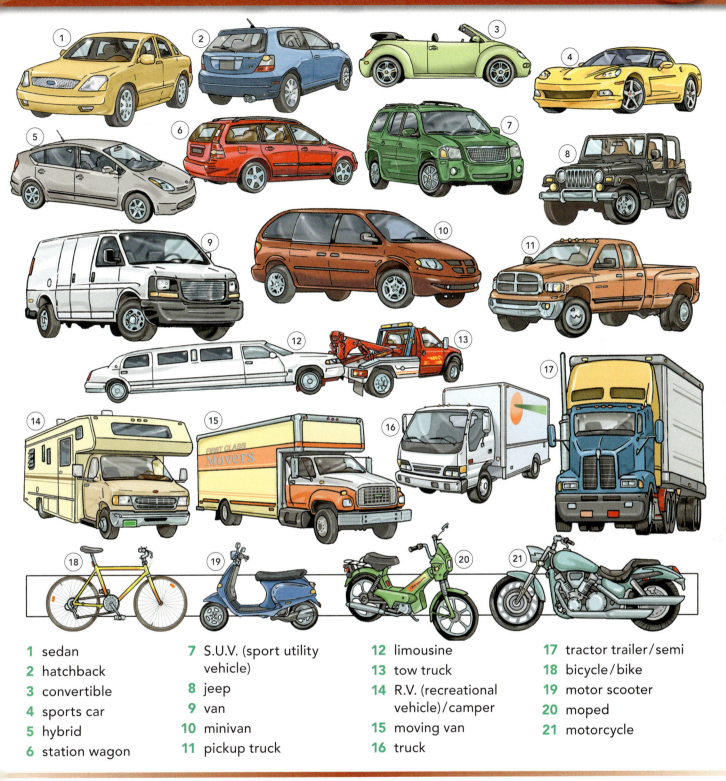

1 sedan
2 hatchback
3 convertible
4 sports car
5 hybrid
6 station wagon

7 S.U.V. (sport utility vehicle)
8 jeep
9 van
10 minivan
11 pickup truck

12 limousine
13 tow truck
14 R.V. (recreational vehicle)/camper
15 moving van
16 truck

17 tractor trailer/semi
18 bicycle/bike
19 motor scooter
20 moped
21 motorcycle

A. What kind of vehicle are you looking for?
B. I'm looking for a **sedan**.

A. Do you drive a/an _____?
B. No. I drive a/an _____.

A. I just saw an accident between a/an _____ and a/an _____!
B. Was anybody hurt?
A. No. Fortunately, nobody was hurt.

What are the most common types of vehicles in your country?

What's your favorite type of vehicle? Why? In your opinion, which company makes the best one?

1 bumper	14 antenna	26 jack	38 alternator
2 headlight	15 rear window	27 spare tire	39 dipstick
3 turn signal	16 rear defroster	28 lug wrench	40 battery
4 parking light	17 trunk	29 flare	41 air pump
5 fender	18 taillight	30 jumper cables	42 gas pump
6 tire	19 brake light	31 spark plugs	43 nozzle
7 hubcap	20 backup light	32 air filter	44 gas cap
8 hood	21 license plate	33 engine	45 gas
9 windshield	22 tailpipe/exhaust pipe	34 fuel injection system	46 oil
10 windshield wipers	23 muffler	35 radiator	47 coolant
11 side mirror	24 transmission	36 radiator hose	48 air
12 roof rack	25 gas tank	37 fan belt	
13 sunroof			

49 air bag
50 visor
51 rearview mirror
52 dashboard / instrument panel
53 temperature gauge
54 gas gauge / fuel gauge
55 speedometer
56 odometer
57 warning lights

58 turn signal
59 steering wheel
60 horn
61 ignition
62 vent
63 navigation system
64 radio
65 CD player
66 heater
67 air conditioning

68 defroster
69 power outlet
70 glove compartment
71 emergency brake
72 brake (pedal)
73 accelerator / gas pedal
74 automatic transmission
75 gearshift
76 manual transmission

77 stickshift
78 clutch
79 door lock
80 door handle
81 shoulder harness
82 armrest
83 headrest
84 seat
85 seat belt

[2, 3, 9–16, 24, 35–39, 49–85]
A. What's the matter with your car?
B. The _____(s) is / are broken.

[45–48]
A. Can I help you?
B. { Yes. My car needs ___[45–47]___.
{ Yes. My tires need ___[48]___.

[1, 2, 4–15, 17–23, 25]
A. I was just in a car accident!
B. Oh, no! Were you hurt?
A. No. But my _____(s) was / were damaged.

In your opinion, what are the most important features to look for when you buy a car?

Do you own a car? What kind? Tell about any repairs your car has needed.

1 tunnel	**9** underpass	**17** broken line	**25** crosswalk
2 bridge	**10** entrance ramp/on ramp	**18** solid line	**26** intersection
3 tollbooth	**11** interstate (highway)	**19** speed limit sign	**27** traffic light/ traffic signal
4 route sign	**12** median	**20** exit (ramp)	**28** corner
5 highway	**13** left lane	**21** exit sign	**29** block
6 road	**14** middle lane/center lane	**22** street	
7 divider/barrier	**15** right lane	**23** one-way street	
8 overpass	**16** shoulder	**24** double yellow line	

[1–28]
A. Where's the accident?
B. It's on/in/at/near the _____.

Describe a highway you travel on.

Describe an intersection near where you live.

In your area, on which highways and streets do most accidents occur? Why are these places dangerous?

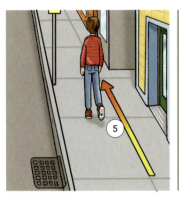

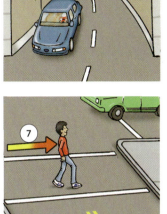

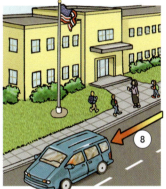
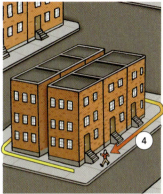
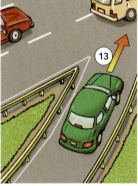

1 over	5 up	9 on
2 under	6 down	10 off
3 through	7 across	11 into
4 around	8 past	12 out of
		13 onto

[1–8]
A. Go **over** the bridge.
B. **Over** the bridge?
A. Yes.

[9–13]
A. I can't talk right now. I'm getting **on** a train.
B. You're getting **on** a train?
A. Yes. I'll call you later.

What places do you go past on your way to school?   Tell how to get to different places from your home or your school.

Traffic Signs

1 stop
2 no left turn
3 no right turn
4 no U-turn
5 right turn only
6 do not enter
7 one way
8 dead end / no outlet

9 pedestrian crossing
10 railroad crossing
11 school crossing
12 merging traffic
13 yield
14 detour
15 slippery when wet
16 handicapped
   parking only

Compass Directions

17 north
18 south
19 west
20 east

Road Test Instructions

21 Turn left.
22 Turn right.
23 Go straight.
24 Parallel park.
25 Make a 3-point turn.
26 Use hand signals.

[1–16]
A. Careful! That sign says "**stop**"!
B. Oh. Thanks.

[17–20]
A. Which way should I go?
B. Go **north**.

[21–26]
A. Turn **right**.
B. Turn **right**?
A. Yes.

Which of these traffic signs are in your neighborhood?
What other traffic signs do you usually see?

Describe any differences between traffic signs in
different countries you know.

A Check-In
1 ticket
2 ticket counter
3 ticket agent
4 suitcase
5 arrival and departure monitor

B Security
6 security checkpoint
7 metal detector
8 security officer
9 X-ray machine
10 carry-on bag

C The Gate
11 check-in counter
12 boarding pass
13 gate
14 boarding area

D Baggage Claim
15 baggage claim (area)
16 baggage carousel
17 baggage
18 baggage cart / luggage cart
19 luggage carrier
20 garment bag
21 baggage claim check

E Customs and Immigration
22 customs
23 customs officer
24 customs declaration form
25 immigration
26 immigration officer
27 passport
28 visa

[2, 3, 5–9, 11, 13–16, 22, 23, 25, 26]
A. Excuse me. Where's the _____?*
B. Right over there.

* With 22 and 25 use: Excuse me. Where's _____?

[1, 4, 10, 12, 17–21, 24, 27, 28]
A. Oh, no! I think I've lost my _____!
B. I'll help you look for it.

Describe an airport you are familiar with. Tell about the check-in area, the security area, the gates, and the baggage claim area.

Have you ever gone through Customs and Immigration? Tell about your experience.

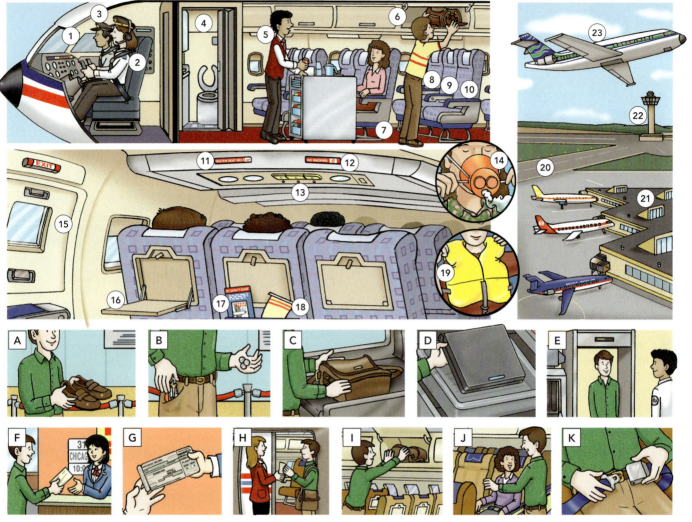

1 cockpit	**10** aisle seat	**18** air sickness bag
2 pilot/captain	**11** Fasten Seat Belt sign	**19** life vest/life jacket
3 co-pilot	**12** No Smoking sign	**20** runway
4 lavatory/bathroom	**13** call button	**21** terminal (building)
5 flight attendant	**14** oxygen mask	**22** control tower
6 overhead compartment	**15** emergency exit	**23** airplane/plane/jet
7 aisle	**16** tray (table)	
8 window seat	**17** emergency instruction card	
9 middle seat		

A take off your shoes	**F** check in at the gate
B empty your pockets	**G** get your boarding pass
C put your bag on the conveyor belt	**H** board the plane
D put your computer in a tray	**I** stow your carry-on bag
E walk through the metal detector	**J** find your seat
	K fasten your seat belt

[1–23]
A. Where's the _____?
B. In/On/Next to/Behind/In front of/Above/Below the _____.

[A–K]
A. Please _____.
B. All right. Certainly.

Have you ever flown in an airplane? Tell about a flight you took.

Be an airport security officer! Give passengers instructions as they go through the security area. Now, be a flight attendant! Give passengers instructions before take-off.

1 doorman	8 front desk	14 meeting room	20 hall / hallway
2 valet parking	9 desk clerk	15 gift shop	21 room key
3 parking attendant	10 guest	16 pool	22 housekeeping cart
4 bellhop	11 concierge desk	17 exercise room	23 housekeeper
5 luggage cart	12 concierge	18 elevator	24 guest room
6 bell captain	13 restaurant	19 ice machine	25 room service
7 lobby			

A. Where do you work?
B. I work at the *Grand* Hotel.
A. What do you do there?
B. I'm a/an _____[1, 3, 4, 6, 9, 12, 23]_____.

A. Excuse me. Where's the _____[1–19, 22, 23]_____ ?
B. Right over there.
A. Thanks.

Tell about a hotel you are familiar with. Describe the place and the people.

In your opinion, which hotel employee has the most interesting job? the most difficult job? Why?

A sew
1 sewing machine
2 pin
3 pin cushion
4 (spool of) thread
5 (sewing) needle
6 thimble
7 safety pin

B knit
8 knitting needle
9 yarn

C crochet
10 crochet hook

D paint
11 paintbrush
12 easel
13 canvas
14 paint
    a oil paint
    b watercolor

E draw
15 sketch book
16 (set of) colored pencils
17 drawing pencil

F do embroidery
18 embroidery

G do needlepoint
19 needlepoint
20 pattern

H do woodworking
21 woodworking kit

I do origami
22 origami paper

J make pottery
23 clay
24 potter's wheel

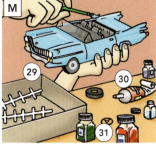

K collect stamps
25 stamp album
26 magnifying glass

L collect coins
27 coin catalog
28 coin collection

M build models
29 model kit
30 glue
31 acrylic paint

N go bird-watching
32 binoculars
33 field guide

O play cards
34 (deck of) cards
   a club
   b diamond
   c heart
   d spade

P play board games
35 chess
36 checkers
37 backgammon
38 Monopoly
   a dice
39 Scrabble

**Q go online/
browse the Web/
"surf" the net**
40 web browser
41 web address/URL

R photography
42 camera

S astronomy
43 telescope

A. What do you like to do
   in your free time?
B. { I like to _____[A–Q]_____.
    { I enjoy _____[R, S]_____.

A. May I help you?
B. Yes, please. I'd like to buy
   (a/an) _____[1–34, 42, 43]_____.

A. What do you want to do?
B. Let's play _____[35–39]_____.
A. Good idea!

Do you like to do any of these activities in your free time?
Which ones?

What games are popular in your country?
Describe how to play one.

1 museum
2 art gallery
3 concert
4 play
5 amusement park
6 historic site
7 national park
8 craft fair
9 yard sale
10 swap meet/flea market
11 park
12 beach
13 mountains
14 aquarium
15 botanical gardens
16 planetarium
17 zoo
18 movies
19 carnival
20 fair

A. What do you want to do today?
B. Let's go to { a/an ___[1–9]___.
              { the ___[10–20]___.

A. What did you do over the weekend?
B. I went to { a/an ___[1–9]___.
            { the ___[10–20]___.

A. What are you going to do on your day off?
B. I'm going to go to { a/an ___[1–9]___.
                      { the ___[10–20]___.

What are some of your favorite places to go? Where are they? What do you do there?

1 bicycle path / bike path / bikeway	**6** picnic table	**12** fountain	**16** playground	**21** seesaw
2 duck pond	**7** water fountain	**13** bike rack	**17** climbing wall	**22** sandbox
3 picnic area	**8** jogging path	**14** merry-go-round / carousel	**18** swings	**23** sand
4 trash can	**9** bench	**15** skateboard ramp	**19** climber	
5 grill	**10** tennis court		**20** slide	
	11 ballfield			

[1–22]
A. Excuse me. Does this park have (a) _____?
B. Yes. Right over there.

[17–23]
A. { Be careful on the ___[17–21]___ !
{ Be careful in the ___[22, 23]___ !
B. I will, Dad / Mom.

Describe a park and playground you are familiar with.

1 lifeguard	7 wave	14 sunbather	21 cooler
2 lifeguard stand	8 surfer	15 sunglasses	22 sun hat
3 life preserver	9 kite	16 (beach) towel	23 sunscreen / sunblock /
4 snack bar / refreshment stand	10 beach chair	17 beach ball	suntan lotion
5 vendor	11 beach umbrella	18 surfboard	24 (beach) blanket
6 swimmer	12 sand castle	19 seashell / shell	25 shovel
	13 boogie board	20 rock	26 pail

[1–26]
A. What a nice beach!
B. It is. Look at all the _____s!

[9–11, 13, 15–18, 21–26]
A. Are you ready for the beach?
B. Almost. I just have to get my _____.

Do you like to go to the beach? Describe your favorite beach. What do you take when you go there?

A **camping**
1 tent
2 sleeping bag
3 tent stakes
4 lantern
5 hatchet
6 camping stove
7 Swiss army knife

8 insect repellent
9 matches

B **hiking**
10 backpack
11 canteen
12 compass
13 trail map

14 GPS device
15 hiking boots

C **rock climbing/
technical climbing**
16 harness
17 rope

D **mountain biking**
18 mountain bike
19 (bike) helmet

E **picnic**
20 (picnic) blanket
21 thermos
22 picnic basket

A. Let's go __[A–E]__ * this weekend.
B. Good idea! We haven't gone
   __[A–E]__ * in a long time.

With E, say: on a picnic.

A. Did you bring
   { the __[1–9, 11–14, 16, 17, 20–22]__ ?
   { your __[10, 15, 18, 19]__ ?
B. Yes, I did.
A. Oh, good.

Have you ever gone camping, hiking, rock climbing, or
mountain biking? Tell about it: What did you do? Where?
What equipment did you use?

Do you like to go on picnics? Where?
What picnic supplies and food do you take with you?

A   jogging
1   jogging suit
2   jogging shoes

B   running
3   running shorts
4   running shoes

C   walking
5   walking shoes

D   inline skating/rollerblading
6   inline skates/rollerblades
7   knee pads

E   cycling/biking
8   bicycle/bike
9   (bicycle/bike) helmet

F   skateboarding
10   skateboard
11   elbow pads

G   bowling
12   bowling ball
13   bowling shoes

H   horseback riding
14   saddle
15   reins
16   stirrups

I   tennis
17   tennis racket
18   tennis ball
19   tennis shorts

J   badminton
20   badminton racket
21   birdie/shuttlecock

K   racquetball
22   safety goggles
23   racquetball
24   racquet

L   table tennis/ ping pong
25   paddle
26   ping pong table
27   net
28   ping pong ball

M golf
29 golf clubs
30 golf ball

N Frisbee
31 Frisbee / flying disc

O billiards / pool
32 pool table
33 pool stick
34 billiard balls

P martial arts
35 black belt

Q gymnastics
36 horse
37 parallel bars
38 mat
39 balance beam
40 trampoline

R weightlifting
41 barbell
42 weights

S archery
43 bow and arrow
44 target

T box
45 boxing gloves
46 (boxing) trunks

U wrestle
47 wrestling uniform
48 (wrestling) mat

V work out / exercise
49 treadmill
50 rowing machine
51 exercise bike
52 universal /
    exercise equipment

[A–V]

A. What do you like to do
    in your free time?

B.   { I like to go __[A–H]__ .
     { I like to play __[I–O]__ .
     { I like to do __[P–S]__ .
     { I like to __[T–V]__ .

[1–52]

A. I really like this / these
    new _____ .

B. It's / They're very nice.

Do you do any of these activities? Which ones?
Which are popular in your country?

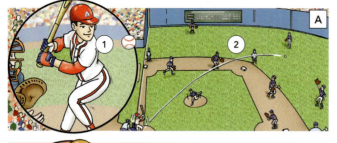

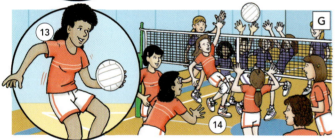

A baseball
1 baseball player
2 baseball field / ballfield

B softball
3 softball player
4 ballfield

C football
5 football player
6 football field

D lacrosse
7 lacrosse player
8 lacrosse field

E (ice) hockey
9 hockey player
10 hockey rink

F basketball
11 basketball player
12 basketball court

G volleyball
13 volleyball player
14 volleyball court

H soccer
15 soccer player
16 soccer field

[A–H]
A. Do you like to play **baseball**?
B. Yes. **Baseball** is one of my favorite sports.

A. .... plays __[A–H]__ very well.
B. You're right. I think he's/she's one of the best _____s* on the team.

*Use 1, 3, 5, 7, 9, 11, 13, 15.

A. Now listen, team! I want all of you to go out on that _____† and play the best game of __[A–H]__ you've ever played!
B. All right, Coach!

† Use 2, 4, 6, 8, 10, 12, 14, 16.

Which sports in this lesson do you like to play? Which do you like to watch?

What are your favorite teams?

Name some famous players of these sports.

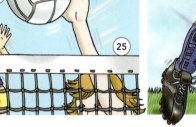

A baseball
1 baseball
2 bat
3 batting helmet
4 (baseball) uniform
5 catcher's mask
6 (baseball) glove
7 catcher's mitt

B softball
8 softball
9 softball glove

C football
10 football
11 football helmet
12 shoulder pads

D lacrosse
13 lacrosse ball
14 face guard
15 lacrosse stick

E (ice) hockey
16 hockey puck
17 hockey stick
18 hockey mask
19 hockey glove
20 hockey skates

F basketball
21 basketball
22 backboard
23 basketball hoop

G volleyball
24 volleyball
25 volleyball net

H soccer
26 soccer ball
27 shinguards

[1–27]
A. I can't find my **baseball**!
B. Look in the closet.*

*closet, basement, garage

[In a store]
A. Excuse me. I'm looking for (a) __[1–27]__.
B. All our __[A–H]__ equipment is over there.
A. Thanks.

[At home]
A. I'm going to play __[A–H]__ after school today.
B. Don't forget your __[1–21, 24, 26, 27]__ !

Which sports in this lesson are popular in your country? Which sports do students play in high school?

A (downhill) skiing
1 skis
2 ski boots
3 bindings
4 (ski) poles

B cross-country skiing
5 cross-country skis

C (ice) skating
6 (ice) skates
7 blade
8 skate guard

D figure skating
9 figure skates

E snowboarding
10 snowboard

F sledding
11 sled
12 sledding dish / saucer

G bobsledding
13 bobsled

H snowmobiling
14 snowmobile

[A–H]
A. What's your favorite winter sport?
B. **Skiing**.

[A–H]
   [At work or at school on Friday]
A. What are you going to do this weekend?
B. I'm going to go _____.

[1–14]
   [On the telephone]
A. Hello. *Sally's* Sporting Goods.
B. Hello. Do you sell _____(s)?
A. Yes, we do. / No, we don't.

Have you ever done any of these activities? Which ones?

Have you ever watched the Winter Olympics? Which event do you think is the most exciting? the most dangerous?

A sailing	**D kayaking**	**F swimming**	**H scuba diving**	**K waterskiing**
1 sailboat	7 kayak	11 swimsuit / bathing suit	17 wet suit	23 water skis
2 life jacket / life vest	8 paddles	12 goggles	18 (air) tank	24 towrope
		13 bathing cap	19 (diving) mask	
B canoeing	**E (white-water) rafting**			**L fishing**
3 canoe		**G snorkeling**	**I surfing**	25 (fishing) rod / pole
4 paddles	9 raft	14 mask	20 surfboard	26 reel
	10 life jacket / life vest	15 snorkel		27 (fishing) line
C rowing		16 fins	**J windsurfing**	28 (fishing) net
5 rowboat			21 sailboard	29 bait
6 oars			22 sail	

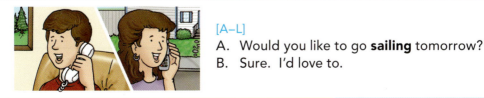

[A–L]
A. Would you like to go **sailing** tomorrow?
B. Sure. I'd love to.

A. Have you ever gone __[A–L]__ ?
B. Yes, I have. / No, I haven't.

A. Do you have everything you need to go __[A–L]__ ?
B. Yes. I have my __[1–29]__ (and my __[1–29]__).
A. Have a good time!

Which sports in this lesson have you tried?
Which sports would you like to try?

Are any of these sports popular in your country? Which ones?

1 hit	7 serve	13 walk	19 swing	25 sit-up
2 pitch	8 bounce	14 run	20 lift	26 deep knee bend
3 throw	9 dribble	15 hop	21 swim	27 jumping jack
4 catch	10 shoot	16 skip	22 dive	28 somersault
5 pass	11 stretch	17 jump	23 shoot	29 cartwheel
6 kick	12 bend	18 reach	24 push-up	30 handstand

[1–10]
A. _____ the ball!
B. Okay, Coach!

[11–23]
A. Now _____!
B. Like this?
A. Yes.

[24–30]
A. Okay, everybody. I want
   you to do twenty _____s!
B. Twenty _____s?!
A. That's right.

Do you exercise regularly?
Which exercises do you do?

Be an exercise instructor! Lead your friends in an exercise
routine using the actions in this lesson.

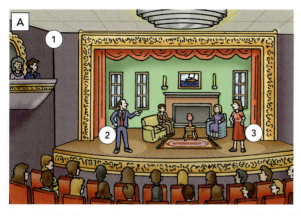

A play
1 theater
2 actor
3 actress

B concert
4 concert hall
5 orchestra
6 musician
7 conductor
8 band

C opera
9 opera singer

D ballet
10 ballet dancer
11 ballerina

E music club
12 singer

F movies
13 (movie) theater
14 (movie) screen
15 actress
16 actor

G comedy club
17 comedian

[A–G]
A. What are you doing this evening?
B. I'm going to { a _____ [A, B, E, G].
the _____ [C, D, F].

[1–17]
A. What a magnificent _____!
B. I agree.

What kinds of entertainment in this lesson do you like?
What kinds of entertainment are popular in your country?

Who are some of your favorite actors? actresses?
musicians? singers? comedians?

A music
1 classical music
2 popular music
3 country music
4 rock music

5 folk music
6 rap music
7 gospel music
8 jazz

9 blues
10 bluegrass
11 hip hop
12 reggae

B plays
13 drama
14 comedy
15 tragedy
16 musical (comedy)

C movies/films

17 drama
18 comedy
19 western
20 mystery
21 musical
22 cartoon
23 documentary

24 action movie/
    adventure movie
25 war movie
26 horror movie
27 science fiction
    movie
28 foreign film

D TV programs

29 drama
30 (situation) comedy/
    sitcom
31 talk show
32 game show/quiz show
33 reality show
34 soap opera

35 cartoon
36 children's program
37 news program
38 sports program
39 nature program
40 shopping program

A. What kind of ___[A–D]___ do you like?
B. { I like ___[1–12]___.
    { I like ___[13–40]___ s.

What's your favorite type of music?
Who is your favorite singer? musician?
musical group?

What kind of movies do you like?
Who are your favorite movie stars?
What are the titles of your favorite movies?

What kind of TV programs do you like?
What are your favorite shows?

Strings
1 violin
2 viola
3 cello
4 bass
5 (acoustic) guitar
6 electric guitar
7 banjo
8 harp

Woodwinds
9 piccolo
10 flute
11 clarinet
12 oboe
13 recorder
14 saxophone
15 bassoon

Brass
16 trumpet
17 trombone
18 French horn
19 tuba

Percussion
20 drums
 a cymbals
21 tambourine
22 xylophone

Keyboard Instruments
23 piano
24 electric keyboard
25 organ

Other Instruments
26 accordion
27 harmonica

A. Do you play a musical instrument?
B. Yes. I play the **violin**.

A. You play the **trumpet** very well.
B. Thank you.

A. What's that noise?!
B. That's my son/daughter practicing the **drums**.

Do you play a musical instrument? Which one?

Which instruments are usually in an orchestra? a marching band? a rock group?

Name and describe typical musical instruments in your country.

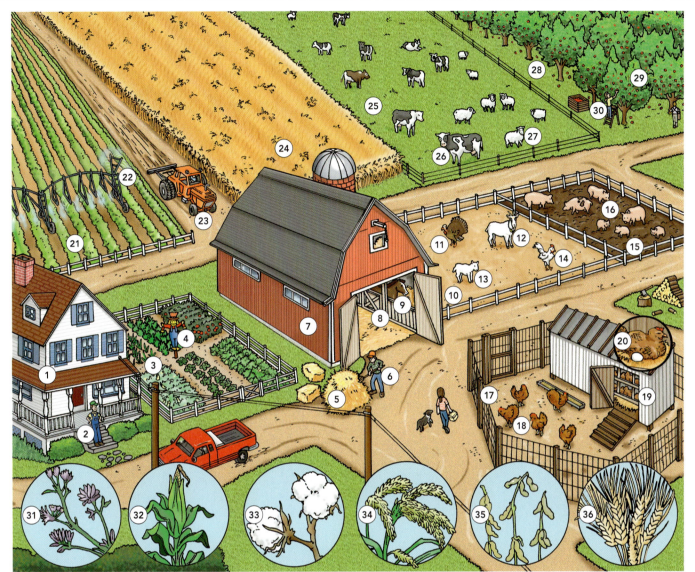

1 farmhouse	9 horse	16 pig	23 tractor	30 farm worker
2 farmer	10 barnyard	17 chicken coop	24 field	31 alfalfa
3 (vegetable) garden	11 turkey	18 chicken	25 pasture	32 corn
4 scarecrow	12 goat	19 hen house	26 cow	33 cotton
5 hay	13 lamb	20 hen	27 sheep	34 rice
6 hired hand	14 rooster	21 crop	28 orchard	35 soybeans
7 barn	15 pig pen	22 irrigation system	29 fruit tree	36 wheat
8 stable				

[1–30]

A. Where's the _____?

B. In / Next to the _____.

A. The [9, 11–14, 16, 18, 20, 26] s / [27] are loose again!

B. Oh, no! Where are they?

A. They're in the
[1, 3, 7, 8, 10, 15, 17, 19, 24, 25, 28] .

[31–36]

A. Do you grow _____ on your farm?

B. No. We grow _____.

Tell about farms in your country. What crops and animals are common on these farms?

1 moose
   a antler
2 polar bear
3 deer
   a hoof-hooves
4 wolf-wolves
   a coat/fur
5 (black) bear
   a claw
6 mountain lion
7 (grizzly) bear

8 buffalo/bison
9 coyote
10 fox
11 skunk
12 porcupine
   a quill
13 rabbit
14 beaver
15 raccoon
16 possum/opossum

17 horse
   a tail
18 pony
19 donkey
20 armadillo
21 bat
22 worm
23 slug
24 monkey
25 anteater
26 llama

27 jaguar
   a spots
28 mouse-mice
29 rat
30 chipmunk
31 squirrel
32 gopher
33 prairie dog
34 cat
   a whiskers

35 kitten
36 dog
37 puppy
38 hamster
39 gerbil
40 guinea pig
41 goldfish
42 canary
43 parakeet

44 antelope	49 panther	53 elephant	56 giraffe	61 gorilla
45 baboon	50 gibbon	a tusk	57 zebra	62 kangaroo
46 rhinoceros	51 tiger	b trunk	a stripes	a pouch
a horn	a paw	54 hyena	58 chimpanzee	63 koala (bear)
47 panda	52 camel	55 lion	59 hippopotamus	64 platypus
48 orangutan	a hump	a mane	60 leopard	

[1–33, 44–64]
A. Look at that _____!
B. Wow! That's the biggest _____ I've ever seen!

[34–43]
A. Do you have a pet?
B. Yes. I have a _____.
A. What's your _____'s name?
B. ....

What animals are there where you live?

Is there a zoo near where you live? What animals does it have?

What are some common pets in your country?

If you could be an animal, which animal would you like to be? Why?

Does your culture have any popular folk tales or children's stories about animals? Tell a story you know.

Birds

1 robin
  a nest
  b egg
2 blue jay
  a wing
  b tail
  c feather
3 cardinal
4 crow
5 seagull
6 woodpecker
  a beak
7 pigeon
8 owl
9 hawk
10 eagle
  a claw
11 swan
12 hummingbird
13 duck
  a bill
14 sparrow
15 goose-geese
16 penguin
17 flamingo
18 crane
19 stork
20 pelican
21 peacock
22 parrot
23 ostrich

Insects

24 fly
25 ladybug
26 firefly/
   lightning bug
27 moth
28 caterpillar
  a cocoon
29 butterfly
30 tick
31 mosquito
32 dragonfly
33 spider
  a web
34 praying mantis
35 wasp
36 bee
  a beehive
37 grasshopper
38 beetle
39 scorpion
40 centipede
41 cricket

[1–41]
A. Is that a/an _____?
B. No. I think it's a/an
   _____.

[24–41]
A. Hold still! There's a _____ on your shirt!
B. Oh! Can you get it off me?
A. There! It's gone!

What birds and insects are there where you live?

Does your culture have any popular folk tales or children's stories about birds or insects? Tell a story you know.

Fish

1 trout
  a fin
  b gill
  c scales
2 flounder
3 tuna
4 swordfish
5 bass
6 shark
7 eel
8 cod
9 ray / stingray
10 sea horse

Sea Animals

11 whale
12 dolphin
13 porpoise
14 jellyfish
15 octopus
  a tentacle
16 seal
17 sea lion
18 otter
19 walrus
  a tusk
20 crab
21 squid
22 snail
23 starfish
24 sea urchin
25 sea anemone

Amphibians and Reptiles

26 tortoise
  a shell
27 turtle
28 alligator
29 crocodile
30 lizard
31 iguana
32 frog
33 newt
34 salamander
35 toad
36 snake
37 rattlesnake
38 boa constrictor
39 cobra

[1–39]
A. Is that a/an _____?
B. No. I think it's a/an _____.

[26–39]
A. Are there any _____s around here?
B. No. But there are lots of _____!

What fish, sea animals, and reptiles can be found in your country? Which ones are endangered and need to be protected? Why?

In your opinion, which ones are the most interesting? the most beautiful? the most dangerous?

1 tree
2 leaf-leaves
3 twig
4 branch
5 limb
6 trunk
7 bark

8 root
9 needle
10 pine cone

11 dogwood
12 holly
13 magnolia

14 elm
15 cherry
16 palm
17 birch
18 maple
19 oak
20 pine

21 redwood
22 (weeping) willow
23 bush
24 holly
25 berries
26 shrub
27 fern

28 plant
29 cactus-cacti
30 vine
31 poison ivy
32 poison sumac
33 poison oak

34 flower	40 chrysanthemum	45 gardenia	50 orchid	55 geranium
35 petal	41 daffodil	46 lily	51 rose	56 violet
36 stem	42 daisy	47 iris	52 sunflower	57 poinsettia
37 bud	43 marigold	48 pansy	53 crocus	58 jasmine
38 thorn	44 carnation	49 petunia	54 tulip	59 hibiscus
39 bulb				

[11–22]
A. What kind of tree is that?
B. I think it's a/an _____ tree.

[31–33]
A. Watch out for the _____ over there!
B. Oh. Thanks for the warning.

[40–57]
A. Look at all the _____s!*
B. They're beautiful!

*With 58 and 59, use: Look at all the ___!

Describe your favorite tree and your favorite flower.

What kinds of trees and flowers grow where you live?

In your country, what flowers do you see at weddings? at funerals? during holidays? in hospital rooms? Tell which flowers people use for different occasions.

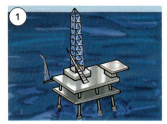
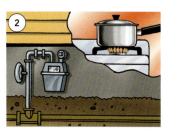

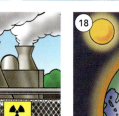

Sources of Energy

1 oil / petroleum
2 (natural) gas
3 coal
4 nuclear energy
5 solar energy
6 hydroelectric power
7 wind
8 geothermal energy

Conservation

9 recycle
10 save energy / conserve energy
11 save water / conserve water
12 carpool

Environmental Problems

13 air pollution
14 water pollution
15 hazardous waste / toxic waste
16 acid rain
17 radiation
18 global warming

[1–8]

A. In my opinion, _____ will be our best source of energy in the future.
B. I disagree. I think our best source of energy will be _____.

[9–12]

A. Do you _____?
B. Yes. I'm very concerned about the environment.

[13–18]

A. Do you worry about the environment?
B. Yes. I'm very concerned about _____.

What kind of energy do you use to heat your home? to cook? In your opinion, which will be the best source of energy in the future?

Do you practice conservation? What do you do to help the environment?

In your opinion, what is the most serious environmental problem in the world today? Why?

1 earthquake	4 blizzard	7 tsunami	9 forest fire	12 mudslide
2 hurricane	5 tornado	8 drought	10 wildfire	13 avalanche
3 typhoon	6 flood		11 landslide	14 volcanic eruption

A. Did you hear about the _____ in .....(country).....?
B. Yes, I did. I saw it on the news.

Have you or someone you know ever experienced a natural disaster? Tell about it.

Which natural disasters sometimes happen where you live? How do people prepare for them?

1 driver's license
2 social security card
3 student I.D. card
4 employee I.D. badge
5 permanent resident card
6 passport
7 visa
8 work permit
9 proof of residence
10 birth certificate

A. May I see your _____?
B. Yes. Here you are.

A. Oh, no! I can't find my _____!
B. I'll help you look for it.
A. Thanks.

Which forms of identification do you have? When do you need to show them?

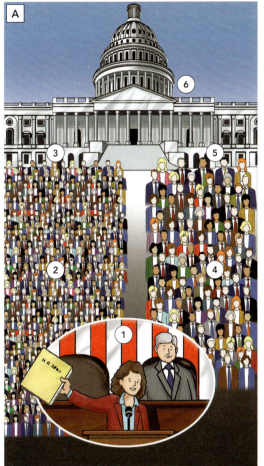

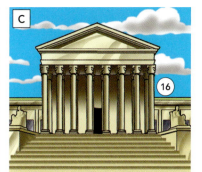

A legislative branch
1 makes the laws
2 representatives /
   congressmen and congresswomen
3 house of representatives
4 senators
5 senate
6 Capitol Building

B executive branch
7 enforces the laws
8 president
9 vice-president
10 cabinet
11 White House

C judicial branch
12 explains the laws
13 Supreme Court justices
14 chief justice
15 Supreme Court
16 Supreme Court Building

A. Which branch of government __[1, 7, 12]__ ?
B. The __[A, B, C]__ .

A. Who works in the __[A, B, C]__ of the government?
B. The __[2, 4, 8–10, 13, 14]__ .

A. Where do/does the __[2, 4, 8–10, 13, 14]__ work?
B. In the __[6, 11, 16]__ .

A. In which branch of the government is the
    __[3, 5, 10, 15]__ ?
B. In the __[A, B, C]__ .

Compare the governments of different countries you are familiar with. What are the branches of government?
Who works there? What do they do?

A The Constitution

1 "the supreme law of the land"
2 the Preamble

B The Bill of Rights

3 the first 10 amendments to the Constitution

C The 1st Amendment

4 freedom of speech
5 freedom of the press
6 freedom of religion
7 freedom of assembly

D Other Amendments

8 ended slavery
9 gave African-Americans the right to vote
10 established income taxes
11 gave women the right to vote
12 gave citizens eighteen years and older the right to vote

A. What is ___[A ,B]___?
B. ___[1 ,3]___.

A. Which amendment guarantees people ___[4–7]___?
B. The 1st Amendment.

A. Which amendment ___[8–12]___?
B. The _____ Amendment.

A. What did the _____ Amendment do?
B. It ___[8–12]___.

Describe how people in your community exercise their 1st Amendment rights. What are some examples of freedom of speech? the press? religion? assembly?

Do you have an idea for a new amendment? Tell about it and why you think it's important.

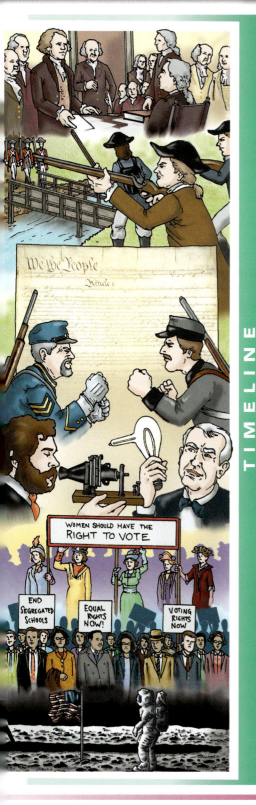

TIMELINE

1607	Colonists come to Jamestown, Virginia.
1620	Pilgrims come to the Plymouth Colony.
1775	The Revolutionary War begins.
1776	The colonies declare their independence.
1783	The Revolutionary War ends.
1787	Representatives write the United States Constitution.
1789	George Washington becomes the first president.
1791	The Bill of Rights is added to the Constitution.
1861	The Civil War begins.
1863	President Lincoln signs the Emancipation Proclamation.
1865	The Civil War ends.
1876	Alexander Graham Bell invents the telephone.
1879	Thomas Edison invents the lightbulb.
1914	World War I (One) begins.
1918	World War I (One) ends.
1920	Women get the right to vote.
1929	The stock market crashes, and the Great Depression begins.
1939	World War II (Two) begins.
1945	World War II (Two) ends.
1950	The Korean War begins.
1953	The Korean War ends.
1954	The civil rights movement begins.
1963	The March on Washington takes place.
1964	The Vietnam War begins.
1969	Astronaut Neil Armstrong lands on the moon.
1973	The Vietnam War ends.
1991	The Persian Gulf War occurs.
2001	The United States is attacked by terrorists.

A. What happened in ......(year)......?
B. ......(Event)......ed.

A. When did ......(event)......?
B. In ......(year)......

In your opinion, which event in this lesson is the most important? Why?

Tell about important events in the history of your country.

1 New Year's Day
2 Martin Luther King, Jr.* Day
3 Valentine's Day

* Jr. = Junior

4 Memorial Day
5 Independence Day/
the Fourth of July
6 Halloween

7 Veterans Day
8 Thanksgiving
9 Christmas

10 Ramadan
11 Kwanzaa
12 Hanukkah

A. When is ___[1, 3, 5, 6, 7, 9]___?
B. It's on ___(date)___.

A. When is ___[2, 4, 8]___?
B. It's in ___(month)___.

A. When does ___[10–12]___ begin this year?
B. It begins on ___(date)___.

Which of these holidays do you celebrate? How?

What holidays do people celebrate in your country?

You have the right to remain silent. 4

$10,000 10

Not Guilty! 20

Guilty! 21

5 years! 22

$100,000 23

A be arrested	**I** go to jail/prison	**8** judge
B be booked at the police station	**J** be released	**9** defendant
		10 bail
C hire a lawyer/ hire an attorney	**1** suspect	**11** courtroom
	2 police officer	**12** prosecuting attorney
D appear in court	**3** handcuffs	**13** witness
E stand* trial	**4** Miranda rights	**14** court reporter
F be acquitted	**5** fingerprints	**15** defense attorney
G be convicted	**6** mug shot/police photo	**16** evidence
H be sentenced	**7** lawyer/attorney	**17** bailiff

18 jury
19 verdict
20 innocent/not guilty
21 guilty
22 sentence
23 fine
24 prison guard
25 convict/prisoner/inmate

*stand-stood

[A–J]
A. Did you hear about ...(name).?
B. No, I didn't.
A. He/She _____ed.
B. Really? I didn't know that.

[A–J]
A. What happened in the last episode?
B. ...(name of character)... _____ed.

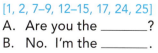

[1, 2, 7–9, 12–15, 17, 24, 25]
A. Are you the _____?
B. No. I'm the _____.

Tell about the legal system in your country.
Describe what happens after a person is arrested.

Do you watch any crime shows on TV? Which ones?
Tell about an episode you remember.

Citizens' Rights and Responsibilities

1 vote
2 obey laws
3 pay taxes
4 serve on a jury
5 be part of community life

6 follow the news to know about current events
7 register with the Selective Service System*

* All males in the United States ages 18 to 26 must register with the Selective Service System.

The Path to Citizenship

8 apply for citizenship
9 learn about U.S. government and history
10 take a citizenship test
11 have a naturalization interview
12 attend a naturalization ceremony
13 recite the Oath of Allegiance

A. Can you name one responsibility of United States citizens?
B. Yes. Citizens should ____[1–7]____ .

A. How is your citizenship application coming along?
B. Very well. I ____[8–11]____ed, and now I'm preparing to ____[9–13]____ .
A. Good luck!

In your opinion, what are the most important rights and responsibilities of all people in their communities?

In your opinion, should non-citizens have all the same rights as citizens? Why or why not?

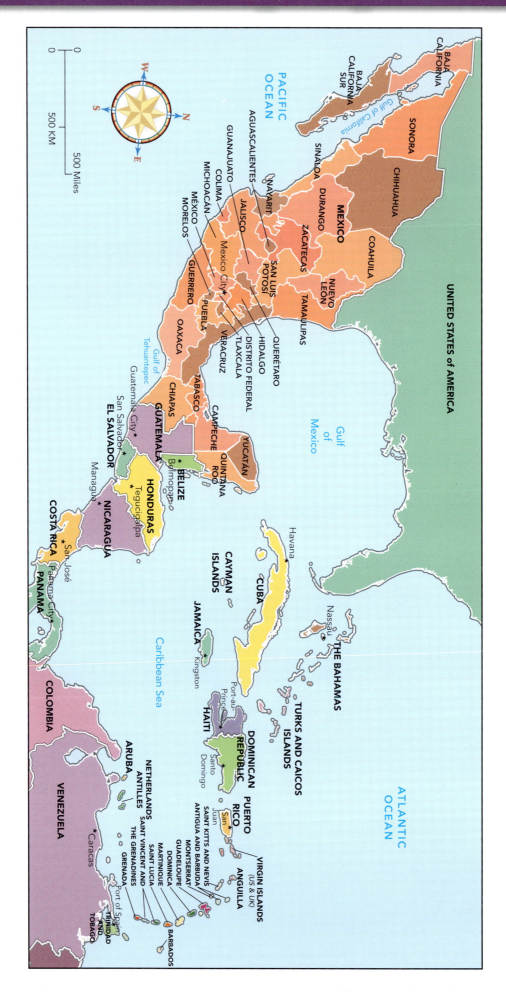

Caribbean Sea

Barranquilla
Cartagena • Maracaibo
Valencia
Barquisimeto ★ Caracas

VENEZUELA

ATLANTIC OCEAN

• Medellín

GUYANA ★ Georgetown
Paramaribo
Cayenne

★ Bogotá

SURINAME FRENCH GUIANA

• Cali

COLOMBIA

Equator

Equator

Quito ★
ECUADOR

• Belém

Guayaquil
Gulf of Guayaquil

Manaus •

PERU

Fortaleza •
Teresina •

BRAZIL

Recife •

• Lima

Salvador •

• La Paz
BOLIVIA

★ Brasília
Goiânia •

Sucre •

Belo Horizonte •

PARAGUAY

Rio de Janeiro •
Campinas •

CHILE

São Paulo •

Asuncion ★

Curitiba •

PACIFIC OCEAN

Pôrto Alegre •

ARGENTINA

• Córdoba

Rosario •

URUGUAY

Santiago ★

Buenos Aires ★
Montevideo •

Gulf of San Matías

ATLANTIC OCEAN

Gulf of San Jorge

N
W   E
S

FALKLAND ISLANDS

Strait of Magellan
Port Stanley

SOUTH GEORGIA ISLAND

0   500 Miles
0   500 KM

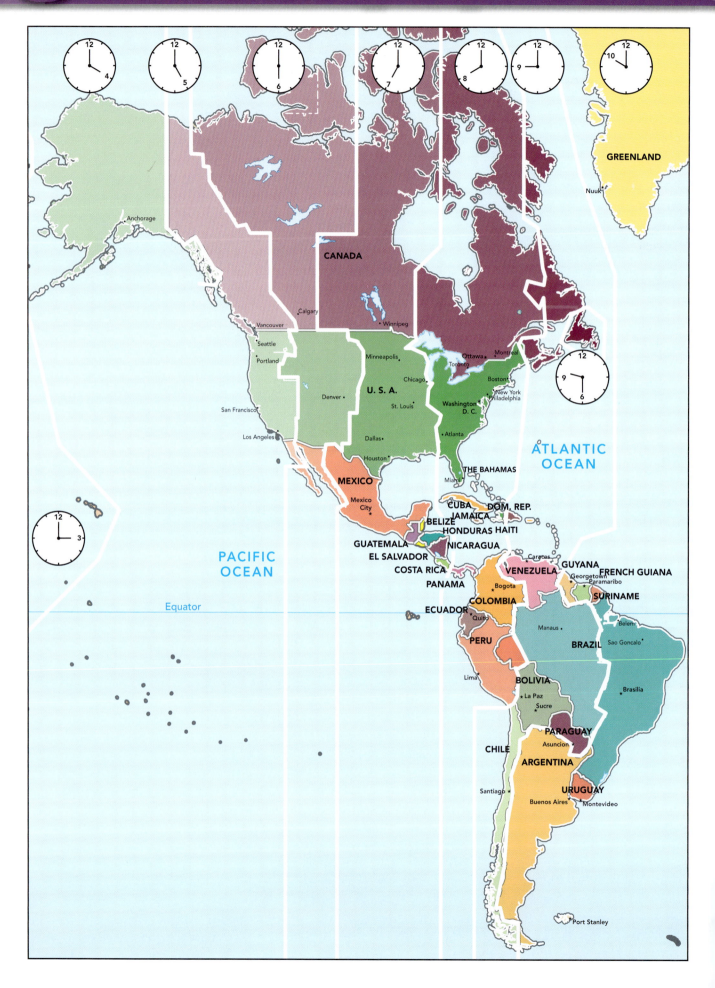

Country	Nationality	Language
Afghanistan	Afghan	Afghan
Argentina	Argentine	Spanish
Australia	Australian	English
Bolivia	Bolivian	Spanish
Brazil	Brazilian	Portuguese
Bulgaria	Bulgarian	Bulgarian
Cambodia	Cambodian	Cambodian
Canada	Canadian	English/French
Chile	Chilean	Spanish
China	Chinese	Chinese
Colombia	Colombian	Spanish
Costa Rica	Costa Rican	Spanish
Cuba	Cuban	Spanish
(The) Czech Republic	Czech	Czech
Denmark	Danish	Danish
(The) Dominican Republic	Dominican	Spanish
Ecuador	Ecuadorian	Spanish
Egypt	Egyptian	Arabic
El Salvador	Salvadorean	Spanish
England	English	English
Estonia	Estonian	Estonian
Ethiopia	Ethiopian	Amharic
Finland	Finnish	Finnish
France	French	French
Germany	German	German
Greece	Greek	Greek
Guatemala	Guatemalan	Spanish
Haiti	Haitian	Haitian Kreyol
Honduras	Honduran	Spanish
Hungary	Hungarian	Hungarian
India	Indian	Hindi
Indonesia	Indonesian	Indonesian
Israel	Israeli	Hebrew

Country	Nationality	Language
Italy	Italian	Italian
Japan	Japanese	Japanese
Jordan	Jordanian	Arabic
Korea	Korean	Korean
Laos	Laotian	Laotian
Latvia	Latvian	Latvian
Lebanon	Lebanese	Arabic
Lithuania	Lithuanian	Lithuanian
Malaysia	Malaysian	Malay
Mexico	Mexican	Spanish
New Zealand	New Zealander	English
Nicaragua	Nicaraguan	Spanish
Norway	Norwegian	Norwegian
Pakistan	Pakistani	Urdu
Panama	Panamanian	Spanish
Peru	Peruvian	Spanish
(The) Philippines	Filipino	Tagalog
Poland	Polish	Polish
Portugal	Portuguese	Portuguese
Puerto Rico	Puerto Rican	Spanish
Romania	Romanian	Romanian
Russia	Russian	Russian
Saudi Arabia	Saudi	Arabic
Slovakia	Slovak	Slovak
Spain	Spanish	Spanish
Sweden	Swedish	Swedish
Switzerland	Swiss	German/French/Italian
Taiwan	Taiwanese	Chinese
Thailand	Thai	Thai
Turkey	Turkish	Turkish
Ukraine	Ukrainian	Ukrainian
(The) United States	American	English
Venezuela	Venezuelan	Spanish
Vietnam	Vietnamese	Vietnamese

A. Where are you from?
B. I'm from **Mexico**.

A. What's your nationality?
B. I'm **Mexican**.

A. What language do you speak?
B. I speak **Spanish**.

Tell about yourself: Where are you from? What's your nationality? What languages do you speak?

Now interview and tell about a friend.

Regular Verbs

Regular verbs have four different spelling patterns for the past and past participle forms.

1   Add **–ed** to the end of the verb. For example:

act → act**ed**

act	cook	grill	pass	simmer
add	correct	guard	peel	sort
answer	cough	hand (in)	plant	spell
appear	cover	help	play	sprain
ask	crash	insert	polish	steam
assist	cross (out)	invent	pour	stow
attack	deliver	iron	print	stretch
attend	deposit	kick	reach	surf
bank	design	land	record	swallow
board	discuss	leak	register	talk
boil	dress	learn	relax	turn
box	drill	lengthen	repair	twist
brainstorm	dust	lift	repeat	unload
broil	edit	listen	request	vacuum
brush	end	load	respond	vomit
burn	enter	look	rest	walk
burp	establish	lower	return	wash
carpool	explain	mark	roast	watch
cash	faint	match	rock	wax
check	fasten	mix	saute	weed
clean	fix	mow	scratch	whiten
clear	floss	obey	seat	work
collect	fold	open	select	
comb	follow	paint	shorten	
construct	form	park	sign	

2   Add **–d** to a verb that ends in **–e**. For example:

assemble → assemble**d**

assemble	declare	grate	pronounce	shave
bake	describe	hire	prune	slice
balance	dislocate	manage	raise	sneeze
barbecue	dive	measure	rake	state
bathe	dribble	microwave	recite	style
bounce	enforce	move	recycle	supervise
browse	erase	nurse	remove	translate
bruise	examine	operate	revise	type
bubble	exchange	organize	rinse	underline
change	exercise	overdose	save	unscramble
circle	experience	practice	scrape	use
close	file	prepare	serve	vote
combine	gargle	produce	share	wheeze

3 Double the final consonant and add **–ed** to the end of the verb. For example:

chop → chop**ped**

chop	mop	skip	transfer
hop	plan	stir	trim
knit	occur	stop	

4 Drop the final –y and add **–ied** to the end of the verb. For example:

apply → appl**ied**

| apply | dry | fry | study |
| copy | empty | stir-fry | try |

Irregular Verbs

The following verbs have irregular past tense and/or past participle forms.

be	was/were	been		know	knew	known
beat	beat	beaten		leave	left	left
become	became	become		let	let	let
bend	bent	bent		make	made	made
begin	began	begun		meet	met	met
bleed	bled	bled		pay	paid	paid
break	broke	broken		put	put	put
bring	brought	brought		read	read	read
build	built	built		rewrite	rewrote	rewritten
buy	bought	bought		ring	rang	rung
catch	caught	caught		run	ran	run
choose	chose	chosen		say	said	said
come	came	come		see	saw	seen
cut	cut	cut		sell	sold	sold
do	did	done		set	set	set
draw	drew	drawn		shoot	shot	shot
drink	drank	drunk		sing	sang	sung
drive	drove	driven		sit	sat	sat
eat	ate	eaten		sleep	slept	slept
fall	fell	fallen		speak	spoke	spoken
feed	fed	fed		stand	stood	stood
fly	flew	flown		sweep	swept	swept
get	got	gotten		swim	swam	swum
give	gave	given		swing	swung	swung
go	went	gone		take	took	taken
grow	grew	grown		teach	taught	taught
hang	hung	hung		throw	threw	thrown
have	had	had		understand	understood	understood
hit	hit	hit		withdraw	withdrew	withdrawn
hold	held	held		write	wrote	written
hurt	hurt	hurt				

The bold number indicates the page(s) on which the word appears. The number that follows indicates the word's location in the illustration and in the word list on the page. For example, "address **1**-5" indicates that the word *address* is on page 1 and is item number 5.

housekeeping cart 133-22
Housewares
  Department 74-10
hubcap 126-7
hula hoop 79-21
humid 14-8
humidifier 94-10
hummingbird 154-12
hump 153-52a
hungry 46-7
hurricane 159-2
hurt 89-44, 91-1
husband 2-1
hybrid 125-5
hydroelectric power 158-6
hydrogen peroxide 90-6
hyena 153-54
hypertension 91-23
hypotenuse 106-19d
hypothesis 110-B

I.D. card 160-3
I.V. 97-6
ice cream 52-18, 60-14,
  64-26
ice cream shop 38-6
ice cream sundae 64-29
ice cream truck 41-28
ice hockey 142-E, 143-E
ice machine 133-19
ice pack 93-16
ice skates 144-6
ice skating 144-C
ice cream scoop 59-1
iced tea 61-18
ideas 107-16,17
ignition 127-61
iguana 155-31
ill 46-4
immigration 131-25
immigration officer 131-26
imperative 107-C
in 8-10
in front of 8-3
in order 7-59
in shock 91-2
inch 106-5
income tax 162-10
independence 163
Independence Day 164-5
index card 120-20
industrial arts 103-15
inexpensive 45-62
infant 42-2
infection 88-10
inflatable pool 79-38
influenza 91-12
information 75-F, 118-B
information booth 124-14
injection 93-14
injured 91-1
ink cartridge 120-26
ink pad 120-28
inline skates 140-6
inline skating 140-D

inmate 165-24
innocent 165-20
insect bite 88-12
insect repellant 139-8
insect spray 33-18
insects 154
insert the ATM card 81-22
instant coffee 51-28
instant message 108-20
instructor 115-30
instrument panel 127-52
insulation 122-25
insurance card 93-3
intercom 25-2, 29-29
international club 104-15
interpreter 115-32
interrogative 107-B
intersection 41-24, 128-26
interstate 128-11
interstate highway 128-11
interview 118-C
into 129-11
invent 163
invitation 108-16
iris 86-9, 157-47
iron 10-4, 73-F,16
ironed clothing 73-19
ironing board 73-17
irrigation system 151-22
is bleeding 90-19e
is choking 90-17c
island 109-19
isn't breathing 90-16b
isosceles triangle 106-20
itchy 89-50

jack 126-26
jacket 66-10,11, 67-4
jackhammer 122-5
jaguar 152-27
jail 40-12, 165-I
jalapeño 49-33
jalapeño pepper 49-33
jam 53-12
janitor 112-20
January 18-13
jar 56-10
jasmine 157-58
jaw 86-15
jazz 148-8
jealous 47-31
jeans 66-6
jeep 125-8
jello 64-27
jelly 53-13
jellyfish 155-14
jersey 66-7
jet 132-23
jewelry box 23-21
Jewelry Counter 74-2
jewelry store 38-7
jigsaw puzzle 79-2
job ad abbreviations 118
job ads 118
job announcement 118-2

job notice 118-2
job search 118
jockey shorts 68-8
jockstrap 68-10
jogging 140-A
jogging path 137-8
jogging shoes 140-2
jogging suit 69-4, 140-1
journal 83-11
journalist 114-1
joystick 78-12
judge 165-8
judicial branch 161-C
juice paks 51-21
juices 51
July 18-19
jump 146-17
jump rope 79-22
jumper 66-21
jumper cables 126-30
jumping jack 146-27
jumpsuit 66-19
June 18-18
jungle 109-15
junior high school 101-3
Jupiter 111-16
jury 165-18, 166-4
justices 161-13

kangaroo 153-62
kayak 145-7
kayaking 145-D
ketchup 53-15, 60-23
key 28-12
key chain 70-17
key ring 70-17
keyboard 5-36, 78-8
keyboard instruments 150
kick 146-6
kiddie pool 79-38
kidnapping 85-7
kidney bean 49-20
kidneys 87-65
kilometer 106-12
kitchen 30-11, 62-15
kitchen chair 24-33
kitchen counter 24-8
kitchen floor 45
kitchen sink 24-12
kitchen table 24-34
kitchen timer 59-24
kite 138-9
kitten 152-35
kiwi 48-9
knee 86-35
knee pads 140-7
knee socks 68-23
knee-high socks 71-9
knee-highs 68-22
knife 22-27, 59-15, 63-34
knit 134-B
knit shirt 66-7
knitting needle 134-8
know about current
  events 166-6

knuckle 87-44
koala 153-63
koala bear 153-63
Korean War 163
Kwanzaa 164-11

lab 97-H
lab technician 97-25
label 75-2
laboratory 97-H
lacrosse 142-D, 143-D
lacrosse ball 143-13
lacrosse field 142-8
lacrosse player 142-7
lacrosse stick 143-15
ladder 122-7
ladies' room 74-16
ladle 59-11
ladybug 154-25
lake 109-6
lamb 151-13
lamb chops 50-7
lamp 21-24, 23-16
lamppost 27-1
lampshade 21-25
land 163
landlord 28-5
landscaper 113-32
landslide 159-11
lantern 139-4
lapel 72
large 44-9, 71-36, 72-5
large intestine 87-60
laryngitis 88-26
last name 1-4
last night 19-11
last week 19-20
latex gloves 123-11
laundromat 38-8
laundry 73-A,G,1
laundry bag 73-5
laundry basket 73-4
laundry detergent 73-7
laundry room 29-45
lavatory 132-4
law school 101-11
lawn 35-A
lawn chair 27-17
lawnmower 27-18, 35-1
laws 161-1,7,12, 166-2
lawyer 114-2, 165-7
LCD screen 78-10
LCD TV 76-3
leaf 156-2
leaf blower 35-15
leaking 30-1, 30-5
learn about U.S.
  government and
  history 166-9
lease 28-6
leather 71-15
leather jacket 67-9
leave a tip 63-G
leave home 10-14
leaves 35-E

left lane **128**-13
leg **86**-33
leg of lamb **50**-6
legal pad **120**-18
leggings **66**-24
legislative branch **161**-A
lemon **48**-20
lemonade **61**-19
length **106**-4, **106**-18a
lengthen **72**-22
lens **77**-15
leopard **153**-60
leotard **69**-12
let out **72**-24
letter **82**-1, **108**-13, **119**-f
letter carrier **82**-28, **114**-4
letter tray **120**-3
letterhead **120**-22
letterhead paper **120**-22
lettuce **49**-9
level **34**-6
librarian **83**-30, **102**-14
library **38**-9, **102**-M
library card **83**-5
library clerk **83**-32
license plate **126**-21
lid **59**-6, **60**-18
life jacket **132**-19, **145**-2,10
life preserver **138**-3
life vest **132**-19, **145**-2,10
lifeguard **138**-1
lifeguard stand **138**-2
lift **146**-20
light **27**-9, **44**-16,26, **72**-12,14
lightbulb **33**-13, **163**
light clothing **73**-2
light green **65**-11
lightbulbs **33**-13
lightening bug **154**-26
lightning **14**-14
lights **7**-42,45
lily **157**-46
lima bean **49**-18
limb **156**-5
lime **48**-21
limousine **125**-12
line **45**, **121**-4, **145**-27
line supervisor **121**-7
line trimmer **35**-3
linen **71**-21
lines **106**
lint trap **73**-12
lion **153**-55
lip **86**-17
lipstick **99**-47
liquid soap **54**-11
liquid vitamins **100**-6
listen to music **11**-3
listen to the answer **6**-20
listen to the question **6**-18
listen to the radio **11**-2
listen to *your* heart **92**-G
liter **56**-22

literary magazine **104**-11
little **44**-10
Little Dipper **111**-3b
liver **50**-9, **87**-57
living room **31**-15
lizard **155**-30
llama **152**-26
load the dryer **73**-D
load the washer **73**-B
loading dock **121**-20
loaf **56**-11
loafers **69**-16
loan **80**-F
lobby **29**, **133**-7
lobster **50**-35
lock **28**-13, **31**-12
locker **102**-Fa
locker room **102**-Ha, **121**-3
locket **70**-10
locksmith **31**-G
lonely **47**-23
long **43**-24, **44**-7, **72**-1
long johns **68**-11
long underwear **68**-11
long-sleeved shirt **71**-1
look at the screen **7**-43
look for an apartment **28**
look in the dictionary **7**-31
look up a word **7**-32
loose **31**-17, **44**-29, **72**-4
lost child **85**-8
lotion **95**-13
loud **44**-45
loudspeaker **4**-14
loveseat **21**-14
low **44**-28, **72**-8
lower the shades **7**-41
low-fat milk **51**-2
lug wrench **126**-28
luggage carrier **131**-19
luggage cart **131**-18, **133**-5
luggage compartment **124**-10
lumber **122**-23
lunar eclipse **111**-8
lunch **9**-16,19
lunchroom monitor **102**-13
lungs **87**-55
lycra shorts **69**-6

macaroni **53**-4
macaroni salad **52**-15
machine **121**-9
machine operator **114**-3
machine screw **34**-29
mad **47**-17
magazine **55**-17, **83**-12
magazine article **108**-10
magazine holder **21**-18
magnet **110**-13
magnifying glass **135**-26
magnolia **156**-13
mail **119**-c
mail carrier **82**-28, **114**-4
mail slot **82**-24

mail truck **82**-29
mailbox **27**-2, **29**-31, **40**-9, **82**-30, **119**-9
mailer **120**-23
mailing address **82**-20
mailing label **120**-24
mailroom **119**-C
main office **102**-A
make a 3-point turn **130**-25
make a deposit **80**-A, **81**-25
make a withdrawal **80**-B
make breakfast **9**-15
make copies **119**-d
make corrections **107**-19
make dinner **9**-17
make lunch **9**-16
make observations **110**-E
make pottery **134**-J
make the bed **9**-10
makes the laws **161**-1
makeup **9**-7, **99**-O
makeup bag **70**-26
mall **39**-23
mallet **34**-2
man **42**-8
manage **116**-16
manager **55**-21, **114**-5
mane **153**-55a
mango **48**-11
manhole **41**-38
manicurist **114**-6
mantel **21**-4
manual transmission **127**-76
map **4**-12
maple **156**-18
March **18**-15
March on Washington **163**
margarine **51**-8
marigold **157**-43
mark the answer sheet **7**-54
marker **5**-34, **79**-26
married **44**-47
Mars **111**-15
martial arts **141**-P
Martin Luther King, Jr. Day **164**-2
mascara **99**-45
mashed potatoes **64**-19
mask **93**-22, **123**-10, **145**-14,19
masking tape **33**-9
mason **112**-10
mat **141**-38,48
match the words **7**-55
matchbox car **79**-14
matches **139**-9
material **71**, **75**-7
maternity dress **66**-18
maternity shop **38**-10
math **103**-1, **105**
mathematics **103**-1

mattress **23**-23, **45**
May **18**-17
mayonnaise **53**-24, **60**-25
mayor **84**-9
meadow **109**-8
meal **62**-D
measles **91**-15
measure *your* height and weight **92**-A
measurements **106**
measuring cup **59**-32
measuring spoon **59**-33
meat **50**
meatloaf **64**-12
mechanic **114**-7
media section **83**-14
median **128**-12
medical assistant **114**-8
medical chart **97**-10
medical history form **93**-4
medical school **101**-12
medicine cabinet **26**-8
medium **71**-35
meeting room **84**-10, **133**-14
melon **48**-16
memo **108**-18
memo pad **120**-8
Memorial Day **164**-4
memory disk **77**-19
Men's Clothing Department **74**-6
men's room **74**-15
menu **62**-8
Mercury **111**-12
merging traffic **130**-12
merry-go-round **137**-14
message **119**-a
message board **119**-29
messenger **114**-9
messy **44**-36
metal detector **131**-7, **132**-E
meteor **111**-9
meter **106**-9, **124**-26
meter maid **40**-17
mice **30**-11g
microfilm **83**-24
microfilm reader **83**-25
microphone **76**-18
microscope **110**-1
microwave **24**-21, **58**-25
microwave oven **24**-21
middle initial **1**-3
middle lane **128**-14
middle school **101**-3
middle seat **132**-9
middle-aged **42**-12
midnight **16**
midwife **97**-20
mile **106**-11
milk **51**-1, **61**-21
milkshake **60**-16
minivan **125**-10

194

Cardinal Numbers

1	one
2	two
3	three
4	four
5	five
6	six
7	seven
8	eight
9	nine
10	ten
11	eleven
12	twelve
13	thirteen
14	fourteen
15	fifteen
16	sixteen
17	seventeen
18	eighteen
19	nineteen
20	twenty
21	twenty-one
22	twenty-two
30	thirty
40	forty
50	fifty
60	sixty
70	seventy
80	eighty
90	ninety
100	one hundred
101	one hundred (and) one
102	one hundred (and) two
1,000	one thousand
10,000	ten thousand
100,000	one hundred thousand
1,000,000	one million
1,000,000,000	one billion

Ordinal Numbers

1st	first
2nd	second
3rd	third
4th	fourth
5th	fifth
6th	sixth
7th	seventh
8th	eighth
9th	ninth
10th	tenth
11th	eleventh
12th	twelfth
13th	thirteenth
14th	fourteenth
15th	fifteenth
16th	sixteenth
17th	seventeenth
18th	eighteenth
19th	nineteenth
20th	twentieth
21st	twenty-first
22nd	twenty-second
30th	thirtieth
40th	fortieth
50th	fiftieth
60th	sixtieth
70th	seventieth
80th	eightieth
90th	ninetieth
100th	one hundredth
101st	one hundred (and) first
102nd	one hundred (and) second
1,000th	one thousandth
10,000th	ten thousandth
100,000th	one hundred thousandth
1,000,000th	one millionth
1,000,000,000th	one billionth

Days of the Week

Sunday
Monday
Tuesday
Wednesday
Thursday
Friday
Saturday

Months of the Year

January	July
February	August
March	September
April	October
May	November
June	December